A Starting-Point Travel Guide

Dijon, France

Including Beaune and the Burgundy Region

Barry Sanders – writing as:

B G Preston

Dijon, France

Copyright © 2025 by B G Preston / Barry Sanders

All rights reserved. No part of this book may be reproduced or transmitted in any form or by any means without written permission from the author via his Facebook page www.Facebook.com/BGPreston.author

ISBN: 9798323698769

3rd edition – Updated April 2025

Acknowledgements: The author greatly appreciates Sandra Sanders' contributions and guidance.

Photography: Maps and photos in the Starting-Point Guides series are a mixture of those by the author, Adobe Media, Shutterstock, Wikimedia, Wikimaps and Google Maps. No photograph or map in this work should be used without checking with the author first.

Contents

Preface & Some Travel Suggestions 1

1: Dijon – The Capital of Burgundy 8

2: Traveling to Dijon 20

3: When to Visit the Burgundy Region 25

4: Where to Stay in Dijon 31

5: Dijon City Pass & Tours 39

6: Transportation in Dijon 44

7: The Owl's Trail 50

8: Dijon Points of Interest 56

9: Beaune – Burgundy's Wine Capital 79

10: Burgundy Vineyards & Wine Route 90

11: Burgundy by Boat & Bicycle 101

12: Nearby Towns to Explore 107

Appendix: Helpful Online References 117

Index 122

Starting-Point Travel Guides 124

Old Town Dijon is a great place to explore and shop.

Preface & Some Travel Suggestions

This Starting-Point guide is intended for travelers who wish to really get to know a city/area and not just make it one quick stop on a tour through France or Europe. Oriented around the concept of using Dijon as a basecamp for several days, this handbook provides guidance on sights both in town and nearby with the goal of allowing you to have a comprehensive experience of this beautiful city and area.

Dijon offers a wealth of historical sights & architecture.

Each of us has varying preferences and what we look for when visiting a new area can differ dramatically. This guide's focus is on orienting you to Dijon and providing highlights on the layout of the town and area and its leading attractions.

This is not an in-depth guide which details every aspect of the history or background of each point of interest. This guide's goal is to ensure you have a better understanding and high-level view of such aspects as: getting around in town, where the sights are, areas to consider lodging and some nearby towns and vineyards to explore.

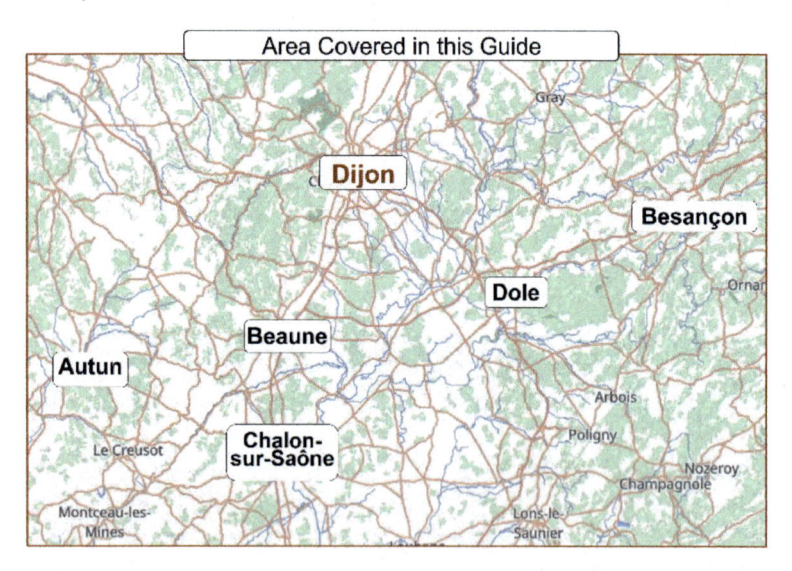

Itinerary Ideas:

The First Suggestion: If your travel schedule allows, plan on staying 2 to 4 nights in Dijon or the nearby town of Beaune. This is an area with a wonderful variety of sights outside of town. Several days are needed to gain even a moderate understanding of what the Burgundy region area has to offer.

The Second Suggestion: Leave one day open and unplanned near the end of your stay. Build in a day in which you have not pre-booked any excursions or planned major activities.

Preface

The reason for this is once there, you will discover places which you either want to revisit or learn of new places which appeal to you. If you have a full schedule, you will lose this luxury.

One Day in Dijon: If your schedule only allows you one full day in Dijon, you can still obtain a wealth of experiences. Depending on your preferences for either learning more about the city, or the area's wines, consider one of the two approaches for your day here:

- **Central City focus & the Owl's Trail:** Spend the full day in the heart of Dijon and walk the "Owl's Trail" which is outlined in chapter 7. Taking all or part of this easy walk leads visitors to many interesting sights which could easily be overlooked without following this trail.

   An alternative to exploring the Owl's Trail (The Owl is Dijon's unofficial symbol), there are many walking tours available which range from self-guided to small groups. Chapter 5 provides help with finding a tour right for you.

- **Head out to Burgundy Wine Country:** Just south of Dijon is the heart of the Burgundy wine region. Many full-day and half-day tours are available out of Dijon which will allow you to enjoy staying in Dijon while also partaking in some great wine tasting.

   Chapter 10 provides guidance on available wine tours and on the Burgundy wine region.

~ ~ ~ ~ ~ ~

Visit the Dijon Office of Tourism: Dijon has two tourist office locations (Office de Tourisme de Dijon). One is in the main train station and the primary office is on the back side of the ducal palace near the Liberation Plaza in the heart of town.[1]

> Dijon Office Of Tourism Website
>
> www.DestinationDijon.com

These offices provide information on available tours and places to visit. Even if you have done substantial research prior to your trip, it is likely you will learn of opportunities which you had not previously uncovered.

Place de la Libération

Tourist Information Center

> The **Tourist Information Center** is located near the Place de la Libération behind the Ducal Palace.

---

[1] **Main Tourist Office Location:** The tourist office (Office de Tourisme) in most cities is easy to find. In the case of Dijon, it is tucked back a bit and behind the city's most prominent building, the Ducal Palace. You may have to ask for directions to find it. The address is: 11 Rue des Forges, 21000 Dijon

Acquire a City Pass from the Tourist Center if you plan on visiting multiple museums or utilize the local transportation system. (See Chapter 5 for details).

Obtain Information on Local Transportation. Dijon has a well-developed transportation network which will enable you to easily move around town.

Understanding the transportation system during a first visit to a city can be daunting at first. The staff at the Office of Tourism will be able to provide help and perhaps sell you tickets to use during your stay. See chapter 6 for details on Dijon's transportation options and how to use them.

Dijon has a comprehensive tram and bus network.

Tour Outside of Town: In almost every European city, there are notable attractions which require a guided tour or train ride to reach them. Dijon is no exception. By checking with the Tourist Office, you will be able to learn of available tours.

With Dijon, the most popular day trips can include a visit to the historic village of Beaune or a tour of the beautiful wine country. See chapters 9 and 10 for details.

In addition to the notable wines of the area, Dijon is surrounded by attractions which meet almost every taste ranging including:

- Large Natural Park – Park Naturel Morvan
- Canals and Rivers with boating excursions. (See chapter 11)
- Large towns and small villages – most are reachable by train. (See chapter 12)
- Biking opportunities through the countryside.

Download Some Apps: With the incredible array of apps for Apple and Android devices, almost every detail you will need to have a great trip is available up to and including where to find public toilets. The following are a few apps used and recommended by the author.

- **Divia Mobilités**: Official app for the local transportation network including bus, trams and bike rentals. A must to help you get around.
- **Dijon Tourist Map Offline**: Very helpful app with detailed maps, info on area attractions and restaurant guide. This firm provides similar apps for many cities.
- **Dijon City Pass:** If you are considering a city pass, this app will help greatly in locating the attractions and shops which are covered. Good level of details and guidance on area attractions.

Dijon Transportation App.
Divia Mobilités
Use for: Bus, Tram, Bike Rental, Parking and Car Rental.

- **Sightseeing Dijon**: (contains ads). Good level of details on local sights, dining and transportation. Very helpful maps.

- **SNCF Connect Trains:** This is the primary regional train service in France. Use this app to see schedules, routes, and purchase rail tickets for travel into Dijon and other cities.
- **Rome2Rio:** An excellent way to research all travel options including rental cars, trains, flying, ferry, and taxi. The app provides the ability to purchase tickets directly online.
- **Trip Advisor:** Probably the best overall app for finding details on most hotels, restaurants, excursions, and attractions.
- **Flush:** A very helpful app which provides guidance on where to find public toilets.

1: Dijon – The Capital of Burgundy[2]

Dijon, the capital of France's Burgundy region, is a pleasant escape from tourism and a delight for history, cuisine, and wine aficionados. The city has been officially labeled as a ***Ville d'art et d'histoire,*** a city of art and history.

This charming city has historical roots dating back to ancient times. In more recent times, it was the capital of the Duchy of Burgundy, and that palace is still prominent in the city center. Throughout the city, there are elements of the city's past in its architecture and historical buildings. If you acquire a map for the ***Owl's Trail,*** this will lead you to several of the historical points of interest in central Dijon. (See chapter 7)

Visitors coming to Dijon will find a small city which is easy to explore on foot as the distances are not great and it is mostly level walking. Most of the historical area's points of interest are within a short walking distance (See chapter 6 for further details). The long pedestrian streets, large parks, and numerous cafes make this a thoroughly pleasant and somewhat laidback place to visit.

Dijons Old Town is a UNESCO World Heritage Site.

Dijon's attractive old city center with its numerous medieval buildings has been designated a UNESCO

---

[2] **Burgundy or Bourgogne:** For simplicity, the English version of "Burgundy" is generally used in this guide instead of the French "Bourgogne." Usage of Bourgogne is limited to specific French names such as the region in which Dijon sits.

World Heritage site. When strolling the winding streets and coming upon buildings representing many different eras, it is easy to see why Dijon was given this designation.

This attractive city is more than wine, mustard [3], and history. It is also an active business, communications, and freight hub strategic importance of this location continues today. Commerce routes date back to Roman times.

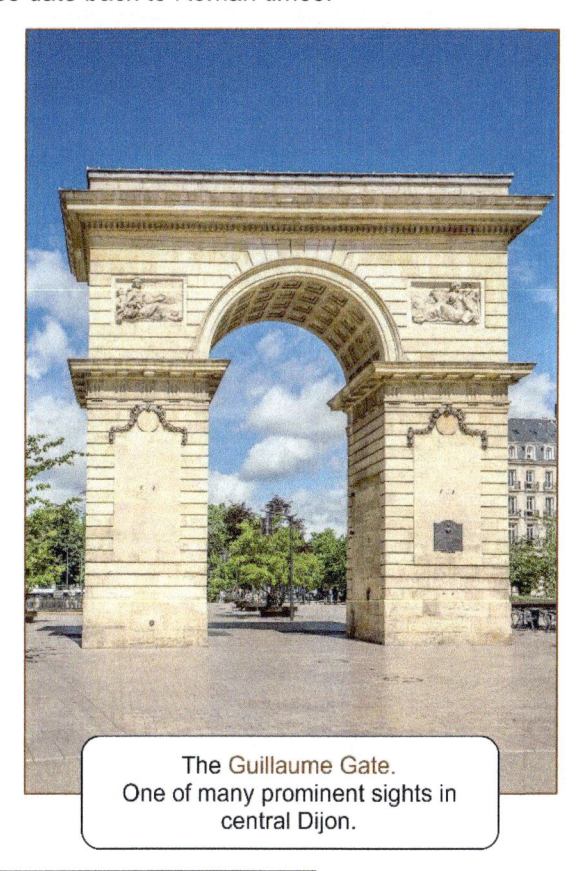

The Guillaume Gate.
One of many prominent sights in central Dijon.

---

[3] **Dijon Mustard:** This popular product is often not produced in the Dijon or Burgundy area. The term "Dijon Mustard" was genericized under European Law and today a majority of the mustard seed is produced internationally.

Dijon's Historic Center: The center of Dijon, where most hotels, museums, shops and other attractions are, is not large. For most visitors, almost every point of interest, including the main train station sits in an area known as *Centre-Ville*. This section of town is less than one mile wide (1.6 km) and less than one-half mile deep.(north-to-south)

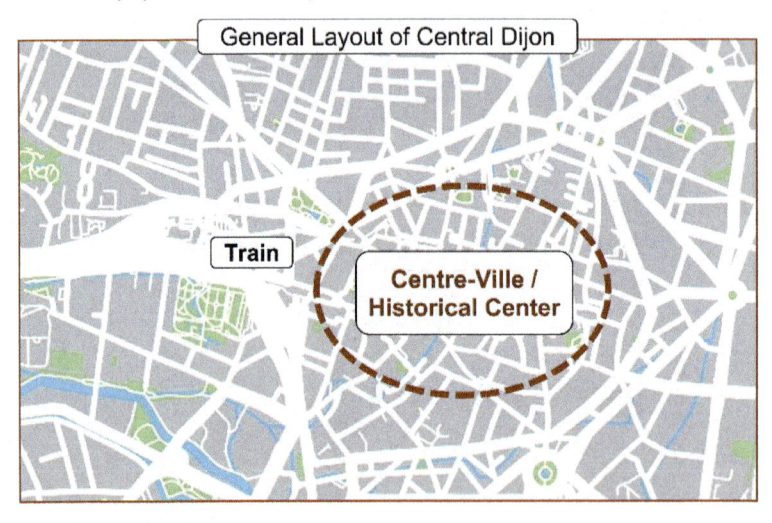

General Layout of Central Dijon

Train

Centre-Ville / Historical Center

Place de la Libération: At the heart of Dijon and the historical center is a large plaza, the Place de la Libération or Place Royale. This square and the adjoining Palace of the Dukes is an ideal spot to start your explorations of this small city. In addition to the palace, the

> This plaza, combined with the palace, adjoining museum and tower are the top "do not miss" sights in Dijon.

Tourist Office is also quite close and there are many enjoyable outdoor restaurants which line the plaza. Standing tall over the palace and plaza is a tower, the Tour Philippe le Bon. This tower is open to visitors and, once you finish your climb to the top, you may obtain great views of the city.

Chapter 8 provides further details on the palace, the tower and this historic plaza.

Restaurants lining **Place de la Libération**
Photo source: Chabe01-Wikimedia Commons

Rivers and Waterways: Dijon differs from many cities in France when it comes to its rivers. Many cities such as Paris, Lyon, Strasbourg, and others have one or more noteworthy rivers flowing through them. In the case of Dijon, the main waterways are not directly in the city center and are not, for most of us, attractions to head to.

There are two small rivers here and one of them, the *Suzon*, is mostly underneath the city. The other river, and adjacent canal, the *Ouche* is a short distance south of town and is generally unappealing. The canal, which is next to the river, will hold interest to individuals who are exploring the area by boat. See Chapter 11 for some more information on exploring the area by canal boat.

Rue de la Liberté
A popular pedestrian shoping street in central Dijon.
Photo source: Chabe01-Wikimedia Commons

Area Names and Identities: Clarification of the identity of the area of Burgundy can be helpful. When reviewing different websites and literature, a variety of names for this region will come up. This variety is due largely to recent consolidation within France of the political divisions.

- **Burgundy or Bourgogne?:** Exactly the same word with Bourgogne being the French version and Burgundy the common anglicized version. Even with the recent merging of some political districts, the use of either of these two terms is still common and acceptable. This guide focuses on the traditional Burgundy area.

Dijon Introduction

- **Bourgogne-Franche-Comté:** In 2015, France consolidated the existing 22 regions into 13. Up until this time, the Bourgogne region stood alone. In 2015, it was merged with the *Franche-Comté* district which sits between Bourgogne and Switzerland. As a result, the use of the longer name is now the official designation.

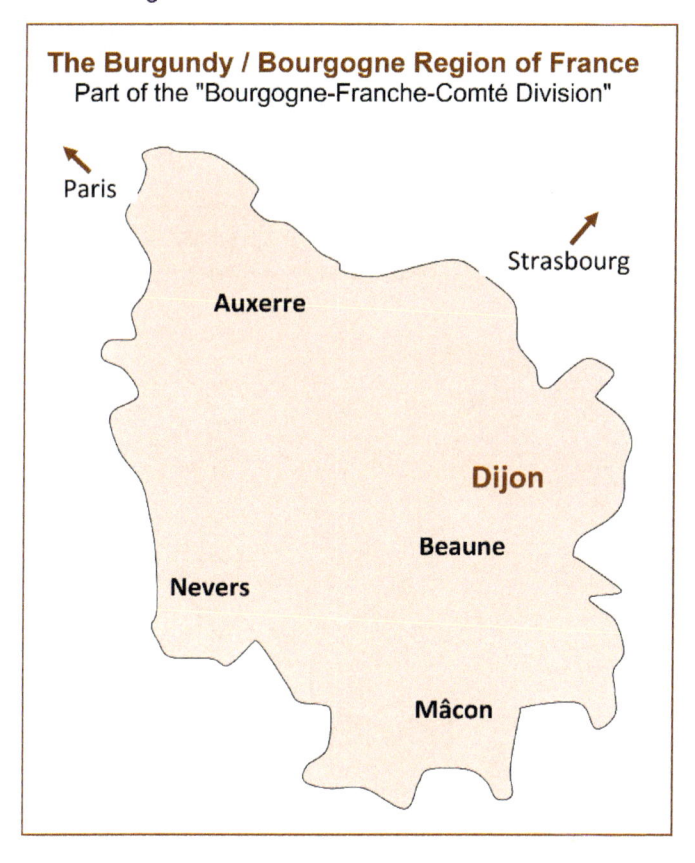

The Burgundy / Bourgogne Region of France
Part of the "Bourgogne-Franche-Comté Division"

↖ Paris

↗ Strasbourg

Auxerre

Dijon

Beaune

Nevers

Mâcon

Dijon Population and Geography:
- The Dijon commune (city proper) has a population of roughly 160,000. The full metropolitan area has over 250,000 people which. This is an active city but one which is not so large as to be overwhelming.

A Starting-Point Guide

- It is France's 17th largest city, putting it well below the larger and more crowded cities such as Paris, Marseille, and Lyon. This ranking changes significantly when looking at overall popularity.

- Situated about 190 miles (300 km) southeast of Paris, Dijon is conveniently located near the rolling hills of the Bordeaux region. The Swiss border is only 93 miles (150 km) further

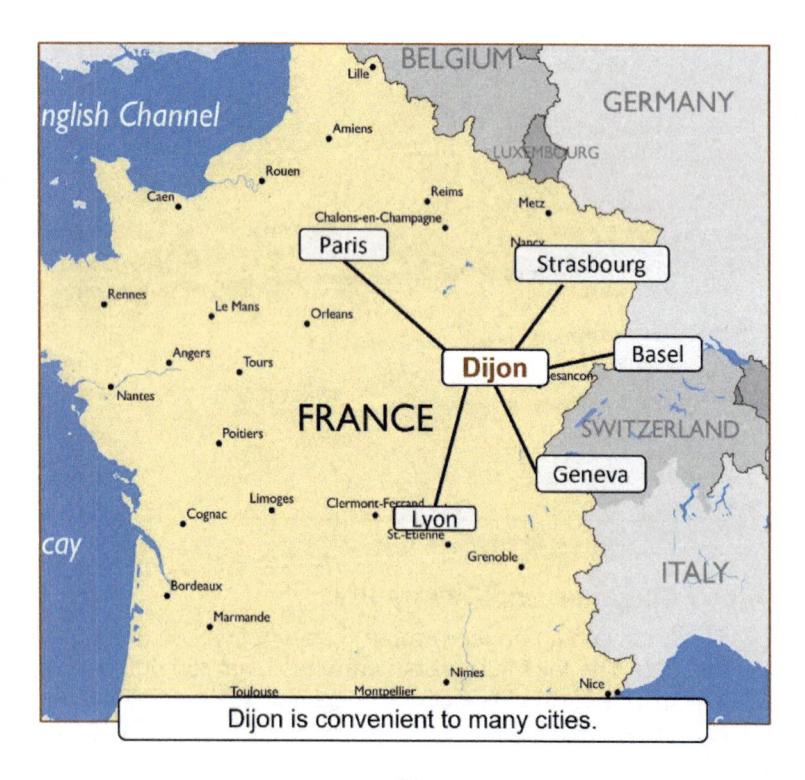

Dijon is convenient to many cities.

14

- southeast. The Swiss cities of Basel and Geneva may easily be reached for a one-day jaunt from Dijon.
- The area surrounding Dijon is a verdant mix of rolling hills with large expanses of farmland. It is this rich farmland which produces not only the famed wines and mustard seeds, but many other crops as well.

Aerial view of Dijon with **Place Darcy** and **William Gate** in the foreground.

History and a Few Interesting Facts:

- **Settlement**: This area was settled as far back as the Neolithic period (about 6,500 years ago). Numerous archeological finds have confirmed this.
- **Romans in Dijon:** The Romans lived here, and the settlement was named Divio. The location between Lyon and Paris was an important stop for commerce.
- **Burgundy Dukes:** During medieval times, the province was the home of the noted Dukes of Burgundy. This family held power here from the 11th through the 15th century. During this reign, its wealth and power grew significantly. A tour through

the noted Ducal Palace in the heart of Dijon is a testament to this.

- **Swiss Invasion:** The city was invaded by the Swiss in 1513 which turned into a violent siege. After a long battle, many locals believed the Swiss were turned away because of a miracle from the Virgin Mary. Because of this, the building of the impressive Notre-Dame Church (Our Lady of Good Hope) was started.
- **Dijon and Major Recent Wars**: Luckily, Dijon was mostly spared from being damaged during major wars such as WWII and the Franco-Prussian War. As a result, most of the city's historic structure remain intact.
- **Dijon Mustard:** The popular Dijon style of mustard (Maille) was created here in 1856 by altering the normal mustard recipe by using verjuice instead of traditional vinegar. Unfortunately, unlike champagne which has been able to hold onto that geographical designator, Dijon mustard can now be produced anywhere.

La Boutique Maille
A popular mustard/moutarde shop in Dijon's historical center.

- **Burgundy Architecture:** During the Gothic and Renaissance periods, a unique "Burgundian" architectural style developed. A distinguishing feature is the multi-colored tile roofs with tiles arranged in geometric patterns. This architecture is still present in many buildings throughout the historical center.

Ornate fountain and sculptures in
Jardin Darcy/Darcy Garden
This park is adjacent to the city's historic center.

- **Mixed Architectural Styles.** Alongside the noted Burgundian architecture, there is a mixture of prominent buildings in Renaissance and Gothic styles.
- **UNESCO Sites:** UNESCO has named Dijon as a World Heritage Site due to the many well-preserved buildings and historic character of this section of town. In addition to the center of town, the neighboring Burgundy wine area has been awarded a UNESCO designation for its unique wine climate.
- **The Dijon Owl:** Owl symbols are common in Dijon and there are carvings on buildings which are over 300 years old. The oldest owl, the Owl of Notre Dame de Dijon, is mounted on the side of the church. It is well worn and most of the details are gone as touching it is thought to bring good luck.

- **Universities:** Dijon is home to several universities and the University of Bourgogne is the largest with 24,000 students. This university is also commonly referred to as the University of Dijon. If you wish to visit the campus it is slightly southeast of the town center.
- **Sports:** If you enjoy sports, consider checking the schedule of JDA FCO. This is a popular soccer (football) team with a midsize stadium known as Stade Gaston Gérard.

Food and Markets: Cuisine and gastronomy play a large role in Dijon and the Burgundy region. From the massive annual **Gastronomic Fair**[4] to the impressive Open Market / *Les Halles,* food is central to the area. There are, unfortunately, no mustard factory tours available anymore, but you can visit delightful mustard shops in the heart of the historic center.

In 2012, Dijon was labeled as an "International City of Gastronomy and Wine" by the French government. To expand on this, a new facility the *Cite de la Gastronomie Dijon* [5] was opened in 2022. This is a large facility which site slightly south of central Dijon and now houses numerous events, classes and shows with a focus on the area's foods and wine.

If you are looking for local food specialties while dining, be sure to try Beef Burgundy for a main dish, snails as an appetizer and gingerbread or snails. For dessert, try some of the local gingerbread.

---

[4] **Dijon Gastronomic Fair:** For details on this popular event, which is held each Fall, (Also known as the Dijon Food Fair), check the website en.DestinationDijon.com for details.

[5] **Cite de la Gastronomie**: The website for this new facility is www.CiteDeLaGastronomie-Dijon.fr

Wine and Châteaux: Two of the great joys for visitors to this region are the world-class wineries and the historic castles or chateaux. Often the two are combined, which makes touring all the more fun.

Château de Commarin
900 year-old castle located 30 minutes west of Dijon
Photo source: ChateauxDeBourgogneFrancheComte.com

Chapter 10 outlines suggestions for visiting several of the more notable vineyards and wine chateaux. Some of these can be reached by train, but most will require use of a car or taking one of the several available tours.

2: Traveling to Dijon

Located southeast of Paris and just west of Switzerland, Dijon's central location is easy to reach. Travel guidance provided here assumes you will be coming by train or car to Dijon or other destinations within the Burgundy region.

> There is **no commercial airport** in or close to Dijon.

Should you choose to drive, this city and area are easy to navigate. This is not a large metropolitan area and there is no maze of busy highways. The streets in and around Dijon are well laid out and highway access into the city is easy to understand.

Arriving by Train: Trains are frequent from neighboring cities such as Paris and Lyon and should be considered if you are booking travel on your own.

Like many cities, Dijon has more than one train station. As of this writing, most trains will bring you to the active *Dijon-Ville* station which is just a short distance from the historical area. Another station, the *Dijon Porte-Neuve,* is less active but more trains, including the TGV[6], are being added. In each case, it is less than a 15-minute walk from the station into the historic district.

When arriving at the *Dijon-Ville station*, you will find several helpful facilities including a small tourist office, restaurants, and car rental. Both tram and bus lines depart directly from the station, making it easy to travel into town.

---

[6] **TGV** – This is France's network of highspeed trains.

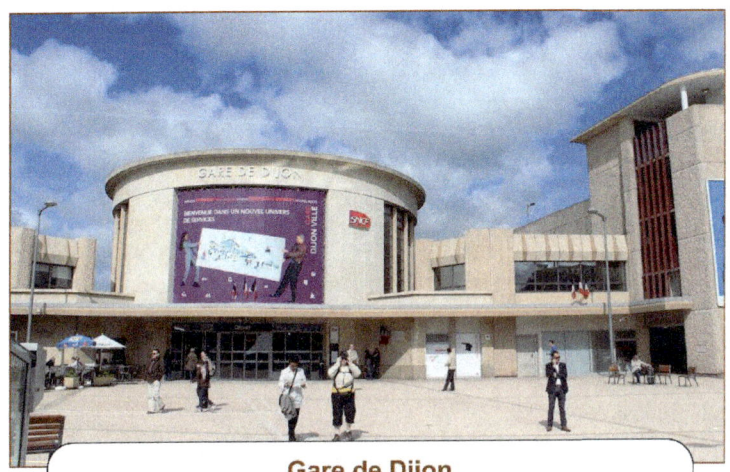

Traveling to Dijon

Gare de Dijon
Dijon's main train station.
Bottom photo depicts tram and bus lines immediately outside of the station.
Photo sources: Christophe Finot and Ketounette-Wikimedia Commons

A Starting-Point Guide

Traveling by Train to Dijon
Typical train travel times from nearby cities.
Data source: rome2Rio.com

Average Train Travel Time to Dijon			
To / From	Travel Time	Trains Per Day	Direct Available?
Basel	80+ Minutes	10+	Yes
Geneva	3 Hours +	8+	No
Lyon	2 Hours	10+	Yes
Paris (City)	90+ Minutes	10+	Yes
Paris Airport (CDG)	2 Hours +	10+	No
Strasbourg	2+ Hours	10+	Yes

Getting from Gare Dijon-Ville into Town

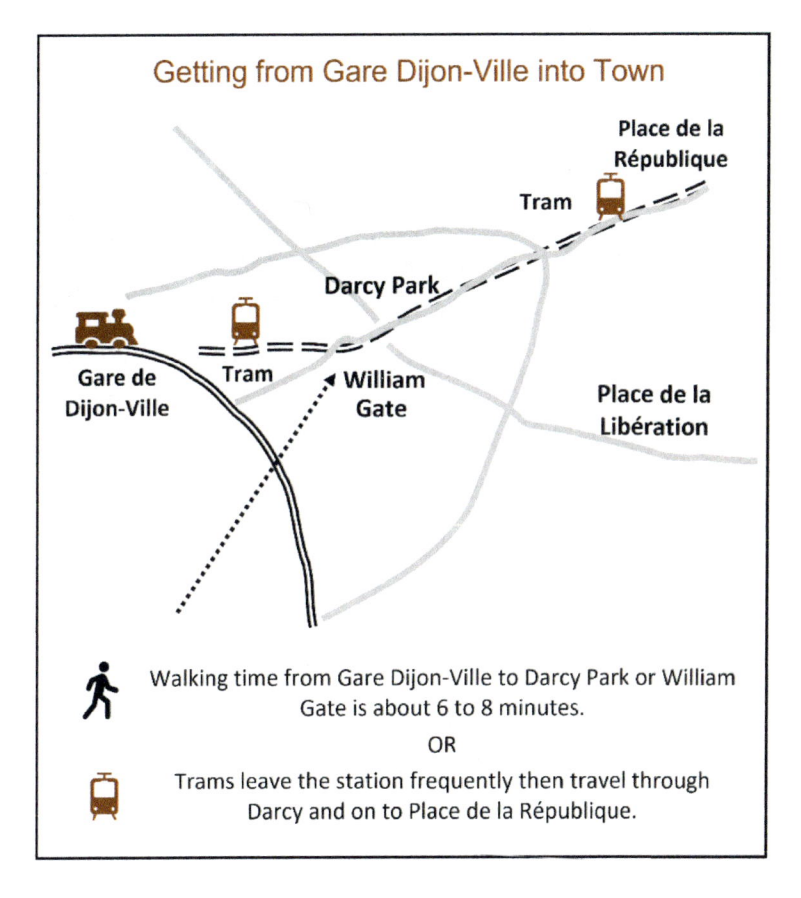

Map showing Gare de Dijon-Ville, Tram stops, Darcy Park, William Gate, Place de la République, and Place de la Libération.

🚶 Walking time from Gare Dijon-Ville to Darcy Park or William Gate is about 6 to 8 minutes.

OR

🚊 Trams leave the station frequently then travel through Darcy and on to Place de la République.

Traveling from Paris by Train: A common route for travelers coming from North America or the U.K. is to travel from Paris to Dijon by train. Two options for departing Paris are available:

From Central Paris: Most of the trains from Paris are high speed TGV and most are non-stop. The trip is typically around 90 minutes.

Most trains from Paris travel to the Dijon-Ville station. A few take you to Porte-Neuve station. Dijon-Ville is recommended due to the greater variety of services, connecting transportation, and proximity to major hotels and attractions in Dijon.

There are several train stations in Paris so it is critical to know which station your train will depart from. When departing Paris, you cannot simply tell a taxi driver to "Take me to the train station."

A TGV High-Speed train

All Dijon-bound TGV trains depart from the **Gare de Lyon** station. This station is in the 12th Arrondissement, a short distance southeast from the center of Paris. Check your booking carefully as a few non-TGV trains depart from Paris to Dijon from other stations.

From Charles de Gaulle Airport (CDG): This is a convenient way to travel as the train station is centrally located in the Paris Airport.

Some trains head directly to Dijon from the airport while others require a change at Gare de Lyon. Take care when booking your train to book a direct train to Dijon to avoid this additional, time-consuming step of changing trains in central Paris.

Booking Train Tickets: Several sources are available to book train travel in France. A few of the leading sources include: (This is not a comprehensive list)

- SNCF.com – The France Rail System
- Rome2Rio.com – an excellent site for comparing and booking most modes of transportation.
- TrainLine.com – a popular site for booking rail travel throughout Europe.

3: When to Visit the Burgundy Region

Like most areas in France, your best times to visit this area are Spring, early Summer, and Fall. This holds true especially if you wish to avoid crowds and enjoy touring, wine harvests, and outdoor activities. In the Fall, the city is much less crowded and has cooler autumn weather.

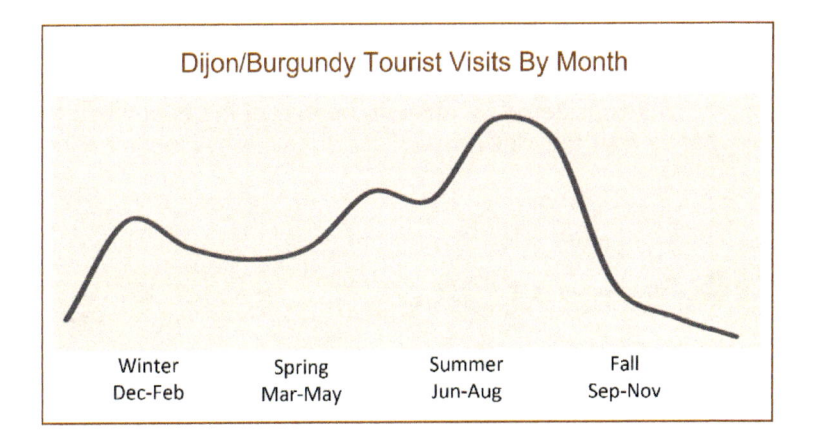

Dijon/Burgundy Tourist Visits By Month

Winter	Spring	Summer	Fall
Dec-Feb	Mar-May	Jun-Aug	Sep-Nov

Dijon sits roughly at 900 feet elevation (275 meters). It is situated in a broad valley with rolling hills to the west and north. The topography leads to a moderate climate for much of the year. Humidity in Spring and Summer is typically in the 50-60% range which is comfortable for most individuals.

The chance of rain is fairly level throughout the year and typically is not bad. Historically, the month with the greatest amount of rain is May, but compared with many cities, it is not bad.

Some Seasonal Considerations:

Winter (Dec – Feb): Temperatures in this region can be cool or cold in the winter along with gloomy and cloudy days. Snow is rare but it does happen on occasion. Many tours are not running. Not a good time to visit vineyards or take tours into the country.

Lack of crowds and lower hotel prices. If you focus on museums and historical monuments, you can have an enjoyable time. Locations, which are packed in the summer months, are open and crowd-free during this time. Most regular stores and shops are open.

Several enjoyable festivals occur during the Winter including the Dijon Christmas Market. For a detailed list of festivals occurring during the time you will be visiting, check www.DestinationDijon.com then go to the Events Calendar under the Practical Information section.

Spring (Mar-May): Few tourist crowds through early May. Temperatures are cool to pleasant. Hotel prices are still low during this time. May is considered by many to be one of the best times of the year to visit the vineyards of Burgundy. Most tours will be

Spring and Summer are great times to take a road trip on the **Route des Grands Crus.**

available to book starting in April. March is still cold with minimal activities. May is typically the wettest month each year.

Summer (Jun-to-Aug): Summer weather in Dijon can be inviting with warm or hot days. This is the time of year when several festivals are held. All tours and tour companies are in full operation along with stores and restaurants. It can be a great time to visit the area's wineries.

July and August can be hot. This is a mixed blessing, depending on your preferences and activities. Tourist crowds are at their height, although tourist crowding here is far less than many other cities in France.

Fall (Sep-Nov): Weather is generally pleasant with cool to warm temperatures. Most shops and tours will be open through October. Hotel rates decrease from their summer highs. Early Fall is a great time to visit the area wineries. Tourist crowds largely disperse, enabling you to enjoy the sights without having to wait in long lines.

November can be cool to cold. Several tours and tourist shops will be closed as the season progresses.

A Great Fall Event!
Dijon's **International Gastronomy Fair** held for 2 weeks in late Oct and early Nov is a huge event for foodies worldwide.

Average Dijon Climate by Month				
Month		**Avg High**	**Avg Low**	**Avg Precip**
Jan	☹	42 F / 6 C	32 F / 0 C	2.2 inches
Feb	☹	46 F / 8 C	32 F /0 C	1.7 inches
Mar	😐	55 F /13 C	37 F /3 C	1.9 inches
Apr	😐	61 F /16 C	41 F /5 C	2.3 inches

Average Dijon Climate by Month

Month		Avg High	Avg Low	Avg Precip
May	😊	68 F /20 C	49 F /9 C	3 inches
Jun	😊	76 F /24 C	55 F /13 C	2.6 inches
Jul	😐	80 F / 27 C	59 F /15 C	2.6 inches
Aug	😐	79 F /26 C	58 F /15 C	2.4 inches
Sep	😊	71 F / 22 C	52 F /11 C	2.2 inches
Oct	😐	61 F /16 C	46 F /8 C	2.9 inches
Nov	😐	50 F /10 C	38 F / 3 C	3.1 inches
Dec	☹	43 F / 6 C	33 F / 1 C	2.4 inches

Major Festivals and Events in Dijon:

There are several popular events in Dijon and the Burgundy wine region each year. Visiting one of these can be a great addition to a tour of the area especially as many of the events put the area's culture and cuisine on display. The only moderate downsides are the added crowds and increased lodging rates for major events. Information on some of the leading events which have broad appeal follows.

Several websites provide a good level of details on upcoming events. The best of these sites is www.DestinationDijon.com. The information is a bit buried in the practical information section but, once you find it, you will find a wealth of information on events small and large.

Winter Events:

- **La Saint-Vincent Tournante:** January, usually around the 3rd weekend of the month. A series of small celebrations throughout the region in honor of Saint-Vincent the patron saint of wine. This is mostly held in the towns in the wine growing region.
- **Christmas Markets:** Almost every city and town have enjoyable Christmas markets which run for most of December. In Dijon, there are numerous celebrations and booths selling crafts and delicacies. This is largely centered around the area between Place Darcy and Rue de la Liberté.

Place de la Libération is a focal point for many of Dijon's Christmas festivities.

Spring/Summer:

- **Festival Art Danse à Dijon:** Lasting several weeks from mid-March to early April is an international festival of dance. This set of events covers everything from traditional ballroom dancing to modern. It is held in several venues across the city so checking the website for details is advised. Website: <u>Art-Danse.Org/Le-Festival.</u>

Fall Festivals:
- **International Gastronomic Fair of Dijon:** (Foire de Dijon) For food lovers, this is a can't miss event. Held during the first half of November in the large "Dijon Congrexpo", an exhibition and convention hall a short distance outside of central Dijon but easy to reach by tram. Details may be found at: <u>www.FoireDeDijon.com.</u>

4: Where to Stay in Dijon

Where you choose to stay when visiting a new city is essentially a personal choice. You may prefer hotels or rental apartments. Picking a place guided by your budget may be critical to you.

Regardless of the motives which drive your selection of accommodation type, the "Where in town should I stay?" question is critical to helping you have an enjoyable visit.

Budget and accommodation-type issues aside, the following criteria may be of importance to you:
- Convenience to historical sites, restaurants, shopping.
- Convenience to transportation.
- Noise levels around where you will stay.

This guide does not provide details on all hotels in Dijon. There are simply too many to describe. There are many fine and dynamic online sources such as Trip Advisor, Booking.com and others which give far more detail than can be provided here. These sites will provide answers to every question about a property you are considering and allow you to make reservations once you have made your selection.

When visiting Dijon, if you remain in or near the historical district or the main train station, this will generally meet the important criteria of transportation and overall convenience.

Dijon or Beaune?

The popular town of Beaune is a good alternative if you wish to get away from the city and stay in a quiet and quaint setting. See chapter 9 for further details on Beaune.

A Starting-Point Guide

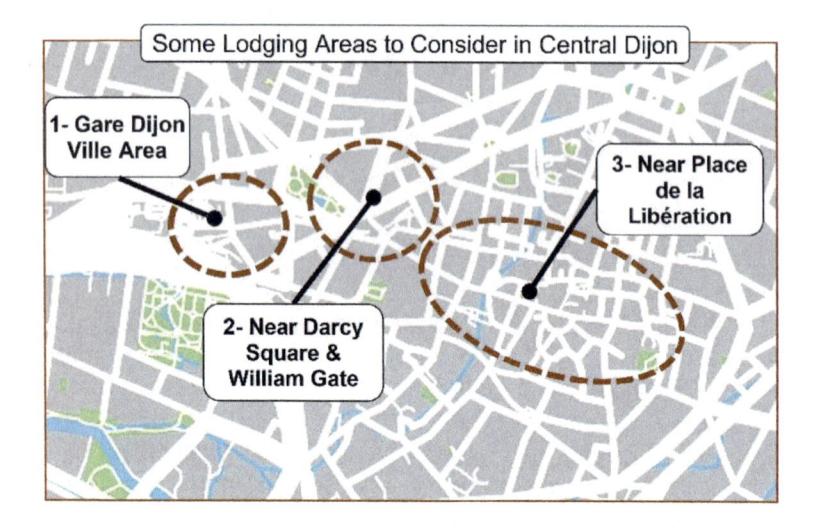

Some Lodging Areas to Consider in Central Dijon

- 1- Gare Dijon Ville Area
- 2- Near Darcy Square & William Gate
- 3- Near Place de la Libération

1-Gare Dijon Ville Area: Several lodging options are near the main train station. In Dijon, the good news is this location is not far from the historical center either.

Positives of staying near Gare Dijon Ville: This area is ideal for travelers to Dijon who are seeking convenience to transportation while not losing access to the main historical area.

If you plan on taking several train excursions out of Dijon or perhaps have an early departure at the end of your stay, considering lodging here is a good choice. If you prefer to walk to the historical area instead of taking a tram, walking times are:

- 7 minutes to Darcy or William Gate

Hotel Oceania le Jura Dijon
4-star hotel just steps from the main train station.

- 15 minutes to Place de la Libération.

Within a few steps from the station and the hotels here are:
- Tram stops for both main lines in Dijon.
- Numerous restaurants and several shops.
- Parking garages.
- Car Rental.

Negatives of staying near Gare Dijon Ville: This is a busy area with substantial traffic from buses, trams, cars, and numerous people walking by. All of this traffic adds to a sense of hectic congestion along with the noise that congestion can bring. The mitigating factor here is that all of the hotels of quality have sound-reducing windows so, unless you are inclined to open a window at night, noise should not be an issue.

Suggested Lodging near Gare Dijon Ville		
(All selected lodgings have 3 star or better rating)		
Hotel	**Address & Details**	**Rating**[7]
Hôtel Oceania le Jura	14 Av. Maréchal Foch Renovated, luxury hotel with a large interior courtyard for relaxing. Full range of amenities including bar, restaurant, fitness center, pool, and business center. Pet friendly. www.OceaniaHotels.com	4 stars
Kyriad Dijon-Gare	7-9 Rue Dr Albert Rémy Immediately across from the train station. Indoor pool, gym, and spa. On-site parking. Pets allowed. Moderate rates. Note, there are two Kyriad hotels in close proximity so take care when booking.	3.5 stars

---

[7] **Lodging Ratings:** All ratings shown in this guide are a composite of the author's own appraisal and leading travel sites. No one specific resource was used.

Suggested Lodging near Gare Dijon Ville		
\multicolumn{3}{c}{(All selected lodgings have 3 star or better rating)}
Hotel	Address & Details	Rating[7]
	www.Dijon-Gare.Kyriad.com	
Kyriad Prestige Dijon Centre	22 Av Maréchal Foch 4 stars Across from the train station. Slightly upscale property with breakfast area and meeting rooms. Visitors here may use the pool and gym at the Kyriad Dijon Gare property which is 1 block away. www.Kyriad.com	

2-Darcy Square & William Gate: This area is often simply referred to as "Darcy." It includes several notable spots of interest:

- **Jardin Darcy/Darcy Park**. A small but attractive city park built over what had once been a reservoir.
- **Place Darcy/Darcy Square.** Small but active square which sits at the entrance to the historic center.
- **Porte Guillaume/William Gate:** Historical monument and archway built in the 1700s. This location sits at the start of the popular pedestrian street, Rue de la Liberté. This street passes by numerous shops and restaurants and leads you to the popular Place de la Libération.
- **Tram Access:** The primary tram lines stop here, providing easy access to the train station, convention center and much of Dijon.

> Recommendation:
>
> For first-time visitors, the Darcy area will be most suitable if your goal is to discover what the historic center of Dijon has to offer.

Darcy Square / Place Darcy
Several quality hotels are adjacent to this popular square.
Photo source: Arnaud 25 - Wikimedia Commons

Positives of staying near Darcy: This area is ideal for anyone who wants easy access to central Dijon and any of the popular attractions.

Within a few steps from the plaza and the hotels are:
- Darcy Garden – an enjoyable place to explore and relax.
- Tram stops for both main lines in Dijon.
- Numerous restaurants and several shops.
- Parking garages.

Negatives of staying near Darcy: Negatives here are few, if any. The hotels in Darcy tend to be more expensive than other areas of town and noise can be a factor.

One of the rooms in the Grand Hôtel La Cloche Dijon

A Starting-Point Guide

Suggested Lodging near Darcy Square/Place Darcy

(All selected lodgings have 3 star or better rating)

Hotel	Address & Details	Rating
Grand Hôtel La Cloche Dijon	14 Pl. Darcy If you have a large budget and enjoy luxury, this is the place to stay. Situated facing Darcy Square, this hotel has every amenity you would want from luxury dining to designer rooms and suites. Room service, spa, parking, and more. All.Accor.com	5 stars
Vertigo Hotel	3 Rue Devosge This unusually named hotel is a short distance from Darcy Garden and plaza. Modern design in the rooms bar and restaurant. Moderate to high price. Facilities include a fitness center, pool, bar, and restaurant. www.VertigoHotelDijon.com	4 Stars
Logis Hôtel Darcy Dijon Centre	1 Rue Dr Maret Tucked away about one block south from Place Darcy. Quiet stretch and easy on the budget. Close to most shopping and attractions. www.Hotel-Darcy.fr	3 stars

~ ~ ~ ~ ~ ~

3- Near Place de la Libération:

In the area of Dukes Place and Place de la Libération, there are several lodging opportunities. Most of these are boutique in nature and each with unique characteristics. This is the section of Dijon to consider staying in if you want to be squarely in the heart of it all. The area differs from other sections of town in that it is highly pedestrian oriented. Cars do travel through most of the streets here, but there are no major thoroughfares.

Positives of staying near the Place de la Libération: Numerous restaurants and shops are just a few steps from your lodging.

- Lively section of town with many events held in Place de la Libération which is next to the Dukes Palace complex.
- Short walk to most of the popular museums and historic sights.

Negatives of staying near Place de la Libération: The negatives here are more oriented to a traveler's personal preferences. For some, being in the busy center will be very appealing, while others may prefer a more sedate location.

- Parking opportunities are limited.
- Noise is often a factor here – although each of the properties listed do have sound-reducing windows.
- No tram service here.
- Greater distance to the train station than other areas listed in this guide.

Suggested Lodging near Place de la Libération		
Hotel	Address & Details	Rating
City Loft	96 Rue des Godrans Hidden away on a side street it would be easy to not realize that this apartment hotel was even there. This property provides small apartments which include a kitchenette. Breakfast buffet is included although there is no restaurant on the property for dinner. www.CityLoftDijon.fr	3.5 stars

Suggested Lodging near Place de la Libération		
Hotel	Address & Details	Rating
Hôtel des Ducs	5 Rue Lamonnoye 3.5 stars One of three properties which are part of the same company and located near the Dukes Palace Complex. The other two are "Maison des Ducs" and the "Résidence des Ducs." www.HotelDesDucs.com	
Hôtel du Palais	23 Rue du Palais 3 stars Located on an unappealing side street, this small boutique hotel offers some pleasant surprises with well-decorated rooms and an enjoyable dining area with wine cellar. www.HotelDuPalais-Dijon.com	
Ibis Styles Dijon Central	3 Pl. Grangier 3.5 Stars Midway between Darcy and Place de la Libération. This is a converted historic mansion with 89 rooms and full-service including bar and restaurant. All.Accor.com	

5: Dijon City Pass & Tours

The City Pass: If you will be staying in Dijon for several days and wish to visit multiple attractions or area wineries (see chapter 8 for list of popular attractions), then acquiring a city pass can be a good idea.

Dijon, like most cities in Europe, offer city passes and they provide discounted or free admissions to many sights.

In addition to admissions to notable attractions, the pass includes free local transportation and discounts to many shops.

The **Dijon City Passes** include unlimited travel on local trams and buses.

Pass Options & Prices:[8] The pass may be purchased in 24- 48- or 72-hour versions. In each case, the pass is good from when it is first used while in Dijon.

City Pass App & Website

Dijon's City Passes may be downloaded as an app for Android and Apple devices. The apps provide additional information on each attraction which can be helpful.

The City Pass website is: DestinationDijon.com. Then go to the City Pass section.

As of April 2025, the online price for an adult pass is as follows:
- 24-Hour: 22€
- 48-Hour: 35€
- 72-Hour: 45€

Printed Passes (best option) may be purchased at the Dijon office of Tourism. You may acquire electronic versions of these passes from www.DestinationDijon.com. The passes are also available through Android and Apple app stores.

What Is Included: The following is a list of several of the attractions and tours included. The items included do change over time so check with the DestinationDijon.com site before purchasing. This is a representative list of inclusions only.

> A **10 € Dijon shopping voucher** is included which will immediately reduce the net cost of these passes if used.

---

[8] **Dijon City Pass Price**: Pricing is subject to change. Check with DestinationDijon.com or the Tourist Office while in Dijon for current pass cost.

Included in the Dijon City Pass – Example Listing

Representative list only. Not all free or discounted locations are shown here as they can and do change.

Item	Pass Benefit
Transportation & Tours Bus and Tram Rides	Free local travel. Not included with the electronic version of the pass.
Bicycle Rental	10% discount
Walking Tour	1 Free guided tour
Museums & Historical Sites:	
International City of Gastronomy	Free visit with gift
La Tour (Tower) Philippe le Bon	Free admission
Musée Magnin (Dijon city museum)	Free admission
Musée des Beaux-Arts (Fine arts)	Free admission
Commarin Castle (35 minutes South of Dijon)	Free castle tour.
Wine / Food / Tastings:	
Cellar Moillard (30 minutes South of Dijon)	Free wine tasting
Château de Meursault (45 minutes South of Dijon)	2 free wine tastings
The Cave of the City (Near central Dijon)	1 free wine tasting
Gingerbread Factory (10 minutes from central Dijon)	Free tour and tasting
Shop Atelier Fallot (Mustard shop)	Free small pot of mustard

Included in the Dijon City Pass – Example Listing	
Representative list only. Not all free or discounted locations are shown here as they can and do change.	
Item	**Pass Benefit**
The Source of Wines – Wine Shop (Wine shop in Dijon)	2 free wine tastings
Vougeot Cellars (30 minutes south of Dijon)	Free tasting
Shopping	
Shopping Voucher	Ten Euro shopping voucher to be used with your choice of participating store.
Tourist Office	5% discount on all items in the store.

Tours in Dijon: Several options for tours in Dijon or out to the neighboring Burgundy wine area are available. Given the modest size of Dijon the array of tours is not as great as in larger cities but still there are tours available to fit most goals.

While many of us prefer to "go it alone" and not join a tour, fitting in one tour, either just a half day or full day, can greatly add to your understanding of an area. In Dijon, a great place to find available tours is the Tourist Center, but this is not your only option. Some tour operators in Dijon include:

Dijon Tourist Office / Office de Tourisme: The tours provided range from short walking tours of the Old Town and historical tours including museum tours. In addition, the Tourist Office provides wine tours and bicycle adventures into wine country and nearby natural parks. The author's favorite is the area cuisine tours and workshops. www.DestinationDijon.com

Major Tour Providers: There are several firms which market and sell tours across numerous cities. In most cases they resell the offerings of local companies, and this provides a level of convenience and customer service which a small agency or guide cannot provide.

For Dijon, browsing the offerings of these firms will present numerous half-day and full-day wine tours, bicycle tours, Dijon city tours and cuisine classes. When researching tours, be sure to check if it is a private tour, small group or large bus operation. Avoid large group tours as you will lose the personal touch and be simply herded along from one locale to the next.

Leading major tour providers include (and are not limited to):

- Get Your Guide: www.GetYourGuide.com. Private and small group tours.
- Viator: A subsidiary of Trip Advisor. www.Viator.com. Private and small group tours.
- Tours By Locals: www.ToursByLocals.com. Most tours are private.

6: Transportation in Dijon
Walking, Trams, and Buses

Dijon is a small city and, as a result, it is easy to navigate and find your way around town. When staying here, there is little need to have a car in town. If you plan on getting out of town to visit the wine country or bike trails in the hillier sections, several rental car companies are available right in town or, better yet, consider joining one of the many tours, especially tours which take you to wine country where you can visit multiple chateaux.

This is an easy town to walk around and explore. It is flat and traffic along most routes is not bothersome. When exploring the historic area, several pedestrian-only streets make it even easier to stroll, have a coffee at a sidewalk café, and find your way to the major sites.

One enjoyable way of exploring the city is to rent a bicycle. Rental stations may be found at the train stations and numerous places throughout the city. Further information on this follows in this chapter.

Local trams and buses are included in the Dijon City Pass.

Almost every location in town can be reached by walking or taking the local trams or buses. The map on the following page provides several examples of normal walking times between leading destinations.

~ ~ ~ ~ ~ ~

Getting Around in Dijon

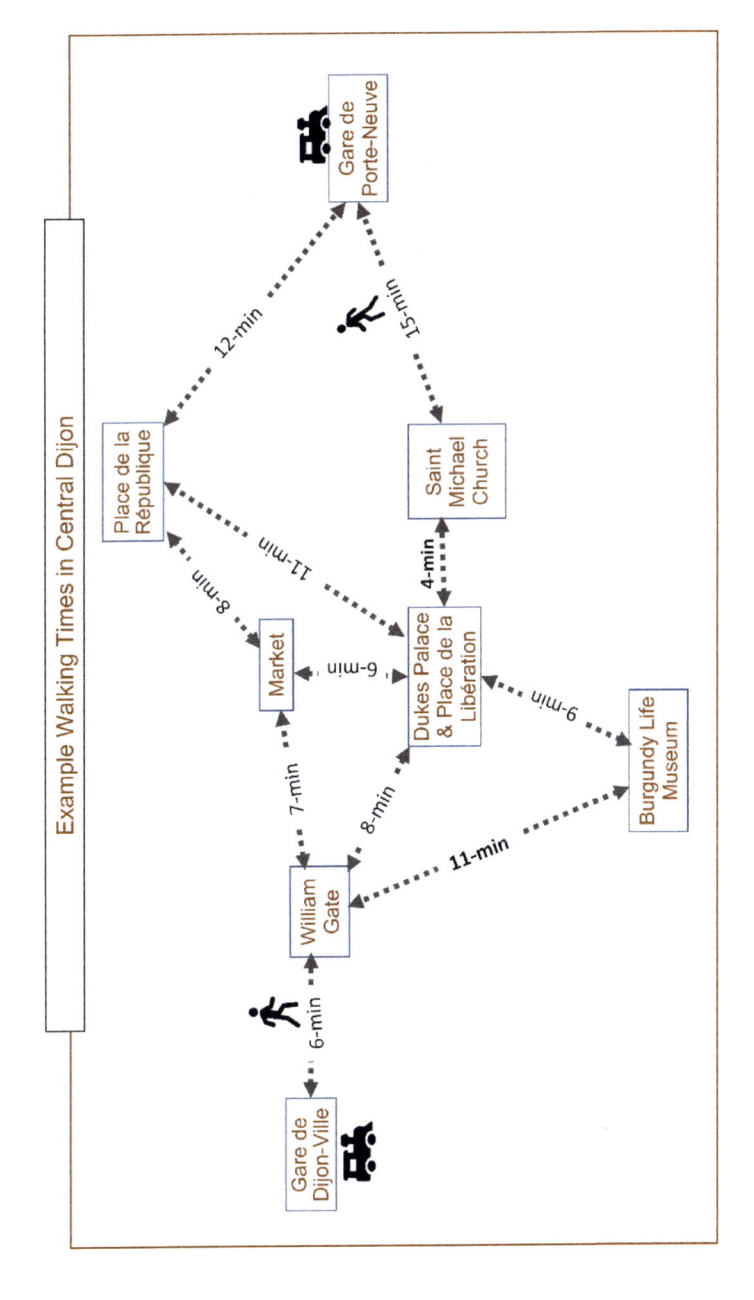

Example Walking Times in Central Dijon

- Gare de Dijon-Ville — 6-min — William Gate
- William Gate — 7-min — Market
- William Gate — 8-min — Dukes Palace & Place de la Libération
- William Gate — 11-min — Burgundy Life Museum
- Market — 8-min — Place de la République
- Market — 6-min — Dukes Palace & Place de la Libération
- Place de la République — 11-min — Dukes Palace & Place de la Libération
- Place de la République — 12-min — Gare de Porte-Neuve
- Dukes Palace & Place de la Libération — 4-min — Saint Michael Church
- Dukes Palace & Place de la Libération — 9-min — Burgundy Life Museum
- Saint Michael Church — 15-min — Gare de Porte-Neuve

A Starting-Point Guide

Trams: The tram network (Tramway de Dijon) is not large, but it is simple to understand and can be of great help when heading to or from the main train station. One interesting aspect of the tram lines is they do not take you into the center of Dijon's Old Town, leaving visitors with a walk of several blocks to reach such locations as Place de la Liberation.

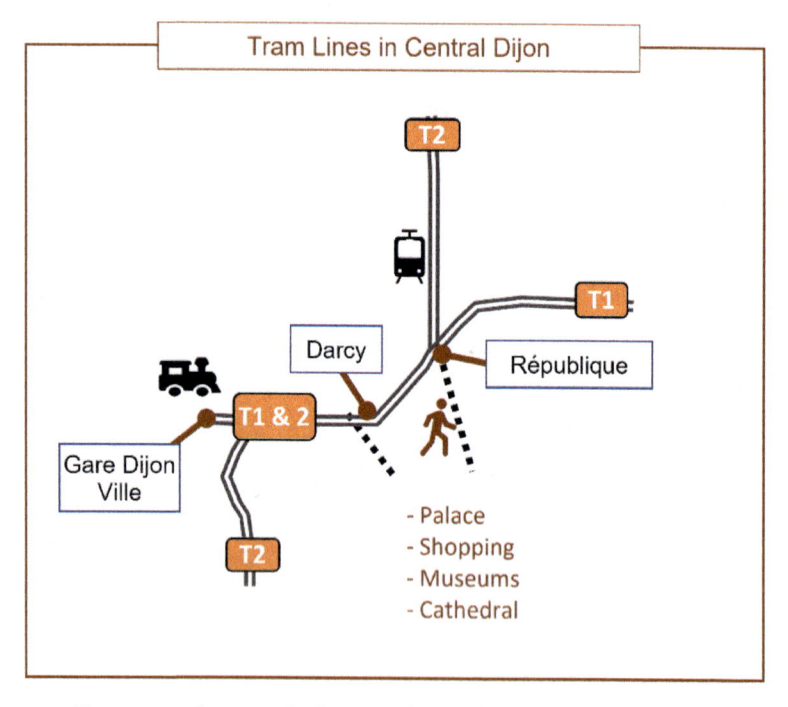

```
                    Tram Lines in Central Dijon

                                    T2

                                    🚋
                                                        T1
                            Darcy
                                              République
        🚂
                         T1 & 2

        Gare Dijon
          Ville                        🚶
                                - Palace
                          T2    - Shopping
                                - Museums
                                - Cathedral
```

Trams run frequently from early morning until 1AM every day. Depending on the time of day, they run between 5 to 15 minutes apart so there is never a long wait for one.

Two tram lines travel through Dijon in something of a T formation. Both lines stop in the following major points:

- Gare de Ville – the major train station
- Darcy – use this stop for the large park, William Gate and ease of access to the central shopping and historical district.

- Godrans – this stop is between Darcy and République and makes a great jumping off point to reach Les Halles, the large open market.
- République - this large plaza is often the site for large events such as the annual Christmas market. From here, the two lines separate with line T-1 heading east to the Exhibition Center where the International Food Fair is held. Line T-2 heads north for several miles into Dijon's suburbs.

Trams do NOT travel to the secondary train station "Gare de Porte-Neuve." To reach this location, it is generally necessary to either walk, take a taxi, or a bus.

Tram and Bus Tickets: When purchasing a ticket to travel on the trams, those tickets work equally well on the buses as this is an integrated network.

Ticket dispensers are at most tram stops and many bus stops. Cash or credit cards may be used. Tickets may also be purchased in several stores throughout Dijon. A list of outlets may be found at www.Divia.fr, the website for Dijon's local transit company.

Many price options for transit tickets exist ranging from a per-use basis to a selected time period. Some examples include: 1, 10 or 20 "voyages" or 24- or 48-hour passes. All of the options are clearly spelled out at the ticket kiosks at every tram stop.

Dijon Transportation App.
Divia Mobilités
Use for: Bus, Tram, Bike Rental, Parking and Car Rental.

Example Ticket Costs: [9]

- By # of Rides/Voyages: 1 ride: 1,70€ / 10 rides 14,30 Euro.
- By Timeframe: 24-hour: 4,50€ / 48-hour 7,65€

When purchasing tickets, you will be given a "Mobigo" printed voucher. This must be used and validated for each leg of a trip to avoid a fine. An electronic reader is present at the entrance of the tram or bus. Simply hold the ticket up to the validating machine until it beeps for it to be properly validated.

Rental Bicycles: Several bicycle rental firms operate in Dijon, Beaune, and the Burgundy region.

In central Dijon, a popular option to consider is *DiviaVélodi*. This service is associated with the same firm which operates the bus and tram system. This is a comprehensive network of 40+ stations in Dijon with hundreds of available bicycles.

You can pick up a bike at one stop and return it to any of the other stops in town. They may be rented for as little as a 24-hour period or up to 7 days. When renting, the first ½ hour is free.

Using the Bike Rental Service:

1. Locate a DiviaVélodi station. This is easy to do by using the Divia.fr website or simply walking around any of the more popular areas of town. An app to locate these sites is also available. Bike rental stations may be found adjacent to most tram stops and in the heart of the historic area which is not served by trams.

One of many **DiviaVélodi** bike rental stations in Dijon.

[9] **Tram and Bus Fares:** Rates cited here are as of April-2025 and are subject to change.

2. <u>Register to use a bike</u>: Each station has a terminal which allows you to register for bike rental. You will need to provide a credit card. In turn, you will be provided with a username and pass code.
Multiple registrations are needed if you plan on renting more than one bicycle.
3. <u>Pick out a Bicycle</u>: Select one of the bikes and press the button for the bike at the rack. Begin your trip.
4. <u>Return the Bicycle:</u> Pick any bike station with an open position. Hang up the bicycle on the rack. Wait for the terminal to beep that it recognizes the return. Done.

7: The Owl's Trail

A Fun Way to Discover Dijon

Often when first visiting a city, it is normal to head straight to the major sights such as a cathedral or museum. In Dijon, the city has crafted a unique way to easily get to and beyond these popular attractions and learn about the history and culture which makes Dijon what it is.

Dijon has embraced the owl (Chouette) as their unofficial symbol. To provide fun along with a bit of a game, they have created **The Owl's Trail** (Le Parcours de la Chouette).

It started with the original owl which had been carved on the side of the cathedral *Église Notre-Dame.* Since then, several more have been added to the current route which includes 22 stops over a 3 kilometer walk through town.[10]

The current trail is marked by a series of plaques on the streets and walkways. Often, these plaques have direction arrows to guide you to the next stop.

Follow the Owl's Trail. A fun self-guided tour of Dijon.

---

[10] **Dijon Points of Interest Details:** The following chapter provides further information on the most notable points of interest in central Dijon. Many of these are also included in the list of stops along the Owl's Trail.

An **Owl's Trail app** is available through your app store for a small fee.

When arriving at a site, a large plaque with a number and often a description will be present.

The Tourist Information Office provides a detailed booklet on the trail. There is a small charge, and it is available in English. The booklet also details additional loops which take you outside of the primary trail.

The trail may be started from any of the 22 points and may be walked in either direction. Not all parts of the route are well marked so having the booklet or the app handy can be helpful.

An Owl's Trail app is available for both Android and Apple devices. There is a small fee to purchase it.

Owls Trail Stops (See following map): The added fun challenge at each stop is locating the actual owl. Some are carved into buildings while others are wall plaques. Details on several of the major destinations included in the Owl's Trail may be found in the following chapter.

1. **Jardin Darcy:** Dijon's first public park which was created in 1880. Look for the prominent "White Bear" statue when visiting here.

2. **Hotel de la Cloche:** A prominent building in Dijon which is over 500 years old.

3. **Porte Guillaume (William Gate):** An 18th century triumphal arch at the entrance to the popular shopping street "Rue de la Liberté."

4. **Poste Office–Grangier Square:** An active square with the "Hôtel des Postes."

A Starting-Point Guide

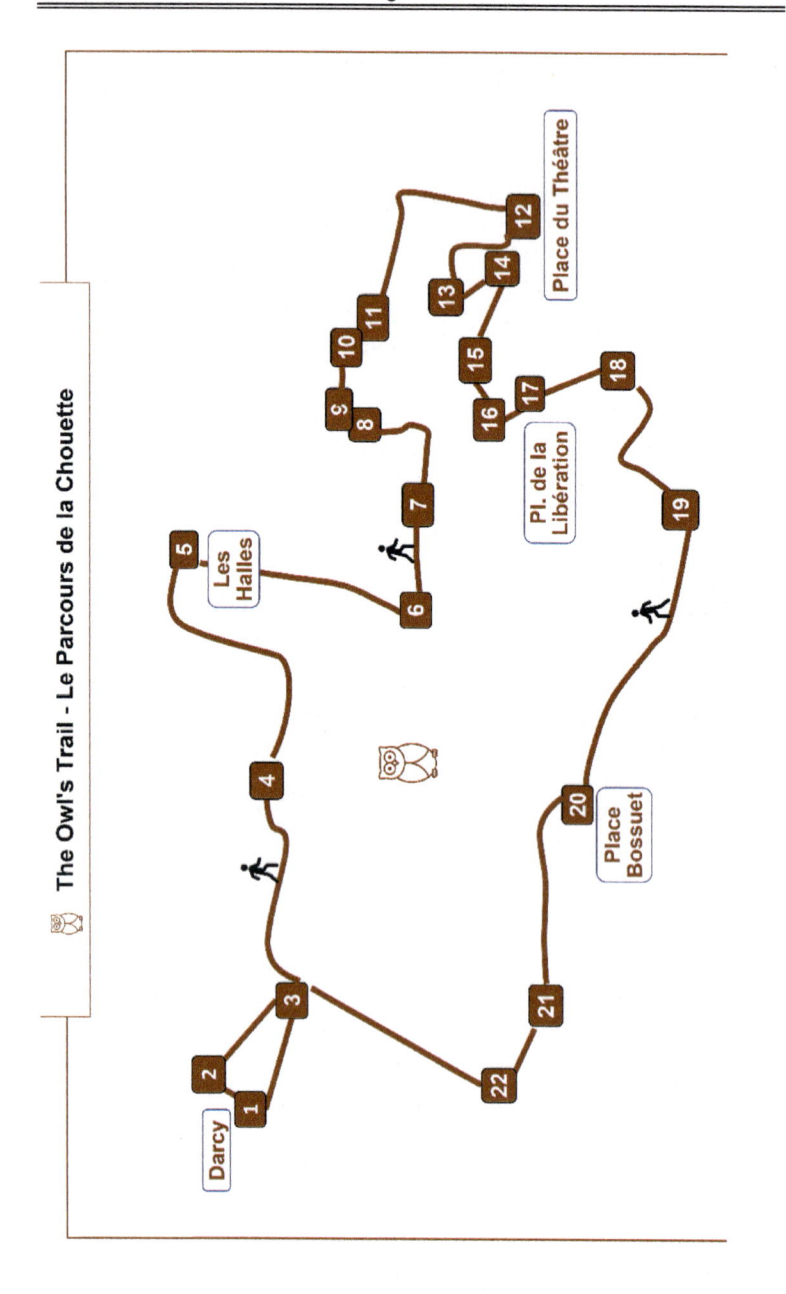

The Owl's Trail - Le Parcours de la Chouette

- Darcy
- Les Halles
- Place du Théâtre
- Pl. de la Libération
- Place Bossuet

52

Les Halles Market
#5 on the Owl's Trail

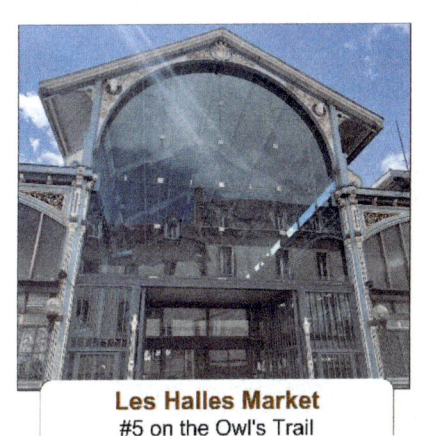

The Owl of Dijon
#9 on the Owl's Trail
Tradition says that if you rub the owl, it will bring you good luck.
Give it a try!

5. **Les Halles-Covered Market:** Large and active market with a wide array of local goods. Open 4 days a week.

6. **Place François Rude:** Head south 2 blocks from Les Halles to find a square with many outdoor restaurants. This square often has local craft fairs and even carnival rides.

7. **Rue des Forges:** Look for the Tourist Office and several upscale shops along this pedestrian street.

8. **Église Notre-Dame de Dijon Cathedral:** Impressive 13th century cathedral.

9. **The Owl of Dijon:** Located on the side of the cathedral. This is the one which started it all and tradition has it, if you rub it with your left hand and make a wish, that wish might come true.

10. **Maison Millière:** House built in 1483 with medieval architecture. Located near the cathedral.

11. **Hôtel de Vogüé**: A great example of a 17th century home.

12. **Place du Théâtre:** Located in the former abbey church. It is a 3-block walk to the south from the hotel and

next to the large library, the "Bibliothèque Centre-Ville."

13. **Square des Ducs (Dukes Square)**: An attractive small park situated on the north side of the large Hotel de Ville.

14. **Musée des Beaux-Arts (Fine Arts Museum):** The Tour de Bar located here was once a medieval dungeon. It is the oldest part of the palace which now houses the fine arts museum.

15. **Palais des Ducs (Dukes Palace):** One of the most prominent buildings in Dijon and a center of the city's history and current activity.

Palais des Ducs (Dukes Palace)
#15 on the Owl's Trail
Photo source: Wikimedia

16. **Tour Philippe le Bon:** Tall tower rising from the center of the Dukes Palace. Take the 316 steps up the tower for great views of Dijon in all directions.

17. **Place de la Libération:** Visit this large semi-circular plaza across from the Dukes Palace. Designed in 1690. Stop in at one of the many outdoor restaurants while looking for owl here.

18. **Palais de Justice:** Situated a short distance south of the Place de la Libération, this impressive structure was designed for the Burgundy parliament in the 16th century.
19. **Historic Mansions and the Legouz de Gerland Hotel**: A block southwest of the Palais de Justice is a collection of narrow streets and notable mansions which had been built for leading members of parliament.
20. **Place Bossuet:** As you work your way west back to the starting point, you will come to the Place Bosseut with several buildings dating back to the early 17th century.
21. **Saint-Philibert Church and Plaza:** This parish of the winegrowers held an important place in the area's politics up until the French Revolution. Visit here now to discover the Archeological Museum situated in the abbey.
22. **Saint-Bénigne:** Across the street from Saint-Philibert is the large Cathédral Saint-Bénigne de Dijon. This is the last stop on the Owl's Trail and a short walk north to where your journey began.

8: Dijon Points of Interest

Top Sights in Central Dijon to Explore

Dijon city's most popular attractions are largely found in the historical center. (The historic & quaint Old Town is, for most visitors, the primary attraction). A few destinations, such as Burgundy Life and Natural History museums are slightly away from the center and a tram ride may be in order.

The map which follows the table below shows the location of the attractions cited here. If you stop in the Tourist Office, you may purchase a larger scale, detailed map of the city. OR consider downloading one of the several available apps such as the Dijon Wiki Map.

\	**Attractions In the City Center**	\
Map#	**Nature of Attraction**	**Name**
1	Plaza	Place de la Libération
2	Tower and Palace	Place des Ducs & Tour Philippe le Bon
3	Art Museum	Beaux Arts Museum
4	Cathedral	Église Notre-Dame
5	Cathedral	Cathédrale Saint-Bénigne
6	Art Museum	Magnin Museum
7	Cultural Museum	Rude Museum
8	History Museum	Museum of Burgundian Life
9	Park	Jardin Darcy

Attractions In the City Center

Map#	Nature of Attraction	Name
10	Plaza & Monument	Place Darcy & William Gate
11	Shopping Street	Rue de la Liberté
12	Mustard Shops	La Maison Maille & La Moutarderie Fallot
13	Open Market	Les Halles
14	Garden & Museum	Natural History Museum & Botanical Garden
15	Food & Wine Experience	Cité International de la Gastronomie et Vin

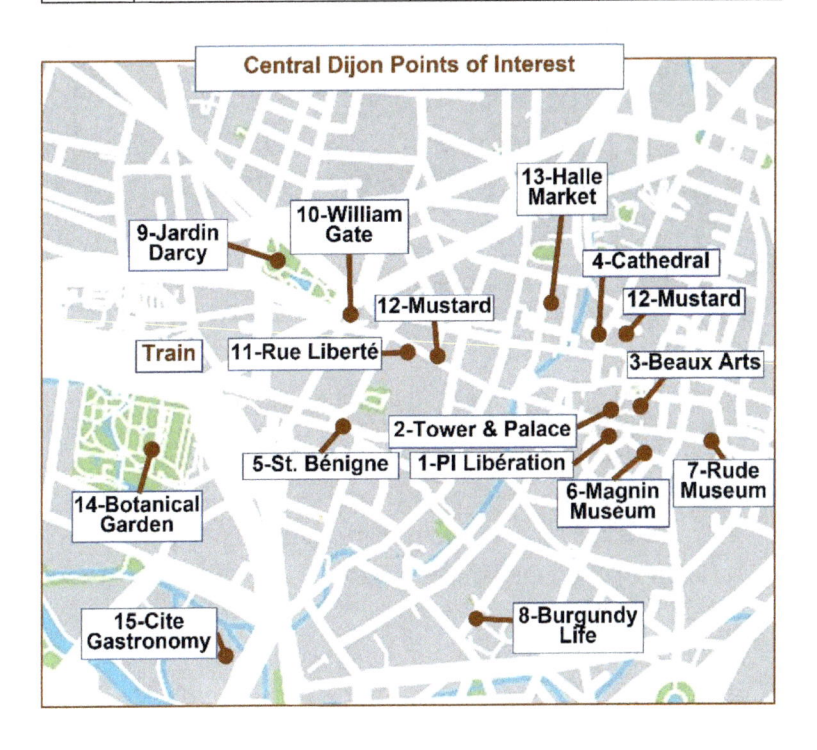

Central Dijon Points of Interest

1 – Liberation Square / Place de la Libération: This half-circle-shaped plaza is the central point for Dijon. The plaza was established late in the 17th century to provide a grand setting for the Palace of the Dukes. In the center of the plaza is a statue of Louis XIV astride a horse. Over its history, the plaza has incurred several name changes. During the late 18th century, it was known as Place d'Armes and, after some restoration, it was named Place Liberation in the 20th century at the end of WWII. This busy plaza wasn't made pedestrian only until 2006.

Place de la Libération
A popular plaza with great photo opportunities.

An interesting aspect of this important plaza is that it is not directly serviced by either the bus or tram systems. The closest bus stop is on the far side of the palace, near the cathedral.
Adjacent to the square are:
- Numerous restaurants, many with outdoor seating.
- Rue de la Liberté, the main shopping street, leads here from Place Darcy.
- The Palais des Ducs.
- Fine arts Museum / Beaux-Arts de Dijon.
- Tour Philippe de Bon – a 15th century tower with views of the city.

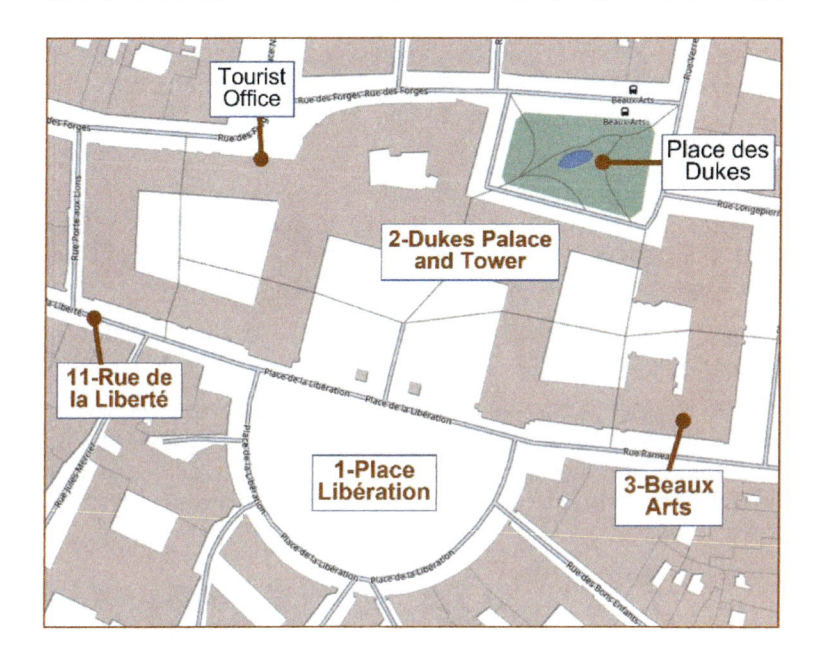

2- Dukes Palace and Tour de Philippe: The most prominent building in Dijon is the Duke's Palace which has the formal name of Palais des Ducs et des États de Bourgogne.

This is a large, complex structure of facilities which was started in the 14th and 15th centuries as a palace. It was finished in the 18th century and the later portions are the most prominent. As a result of construction spanning several centuries, several architectural styles are evident. The oldest parts of this complex are Gothic while the newer sections are in the classical style.

It was built as a royal residence to house the estates of Burgundy. The Duchy of Burgundy dates as far back as the 5th century.

Where: It is located at the central and popular Place de la Libération (Liberation Plaza) which is located at the southern and main entrance to the palace. On the northern side of the palace is the smaller Dukes Square. (Dukes Square is the closest bus stop.)

What is Here: This complex houses several notable sites listed below. Though not all areas are open to the public, there is more than enough to fill a couple of hours of exploring.

Tourist Office (Office de Tourisme): Located at the back of the main building and facing the historic Rue des Forges. Come here to obtain information on all attractions in and around Dijon. Several tour options are available to book here, and the Dijon City Pass may be purchased here. www.DestinationDijon.com

Dijon City Hall (Hôtel de Ville): This is an active city hall and is not normally open for tours.

Dukes Palace: A small part of the palace is available to visit as much of the building houses the city hall and the large Beaux Arts museum. Enter through the Tourist Office where you will be able to view the impressive chapel, 14th century murals and ornate royal tombs.

Tour Philippe (Tour Philippe le Bon): This tower was built in the 15th century and rises nearly 150 feet (46 meters). It is also referred to as "the Philip the Good Tower." To reach the top a climb of over 300 steps is required as there is no elevator.

This is a popular attraction and tickets are required and wait times are likely. The best way to obtain a ticket is to visit the neighboring Tourist Office. A limited number of individuals are allowed up at any one time so the ticket will be for a specific time. There is a small

Tour Philippe le Bon
Philip the Good Tower

fee, unless you have a Dijon City Pass which covers the cost of entering the tower. Closed on Mondays. No restrooms are available at the top.

Website: Get full details on the Tourist Office website at: www.DestinaionDijon.com. Then go to the "destination" and "history and heritage" section of the website.

3- Fine Arts Museum / Musée des Beaux-Arts: This is one of the oldest museums in France. This expansive arts museum opened in 1787 and recently underwent a comprehensive renovation. It now displays over 1,500 works spread throughout 50 different galleries.

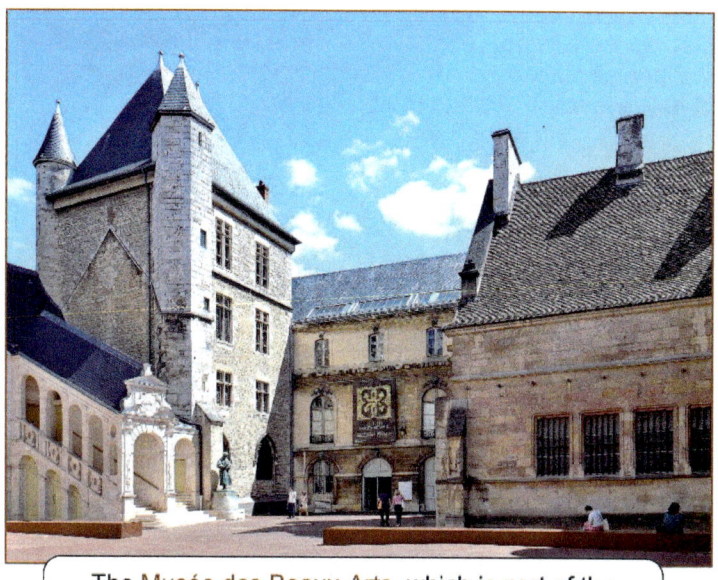

The Musée des Beaux-Arts, which is part of the Palais des Ducs complex.
Photo Source: Patrick - Wikimedia Commons

Notable collections include tombs of the Dukes of Burgundy in addition to a broad range of sculptures and paintings. The collections range from Egyptian and Roman antiquities to the Renaissance era. There is even a collection of contemporary art.

Where: Located inside Dukes Palace / Palais des Ducs.

Entrance Fee: Free admission to most permanent galleries. Guided tours are an additional fee.

When Open: Closed Tuesday. Open all other days except holidays from 10AM to 6PM.

Website: beaux-arts.dijon.fr

Tombs of the Dukes of Burgundy
Photo source: Twibo2-Wikipedia

Numerous works by noted artists such as Monet are included in the collections.

4-Notre-Dame Dijon / Église Notre-Dame de Dijon: This

is a Roman Catholic church considered to be a notable example of 13th-century Gothic architecture. Located near the Dukes Palace and had been used by residents of the palace. It is the oldest church in Dijon.

The church (this is not officially a cathedral) was built in a section which had little room for expansive designs such as flying buttresses which were popular during this period.

The interior is in a traditional Latin cross floor plan and has six tall arcades which are supported by cylindrical columns. One item of interest is the statue called "Notre-Dame de Bon-Espoir" (Our Lady of Good Hope).

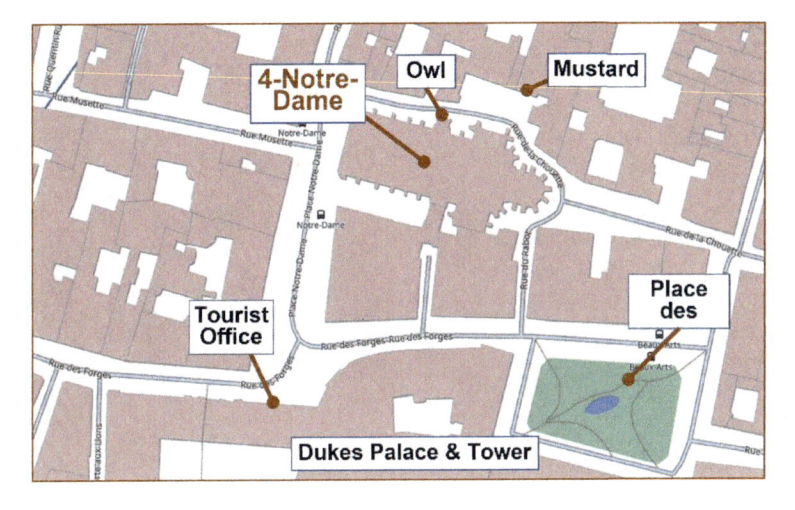

Notre-Dame Dijon
A 13th century Gothic masterpiece tucked away in the historic district.

This statue dates back to the 11th century and is considered to be one of the oldest in France. On the exterior, there are 51 decorative gargoyles and the *Owl of Dijon*.

Cost: No charge to visit this church.

When Open: Every day except legal holidays from 9AM to 6:30PM.

Facilities: There are no restaurants or public restrooms in this church.

Website: www.Notre-Dame-Dijon.Blogspot.com

5-Dijon Cathedral / Cathédrale Saint-Bénigne de Dijon:

This is a Roman Catholic cathedral built during the 13th and 14th centuries. It is the tallest building in Dijon and houses the grave of the Duke of Burgundy, Philip III. The large building includes an impressive basilica which is built over an expansive crypt which dates to the 6th century.

The building has encountered several disasters over the years including a fire which destroyed much of the building along with much of Dijon in 1137. In the 13th century, a tall

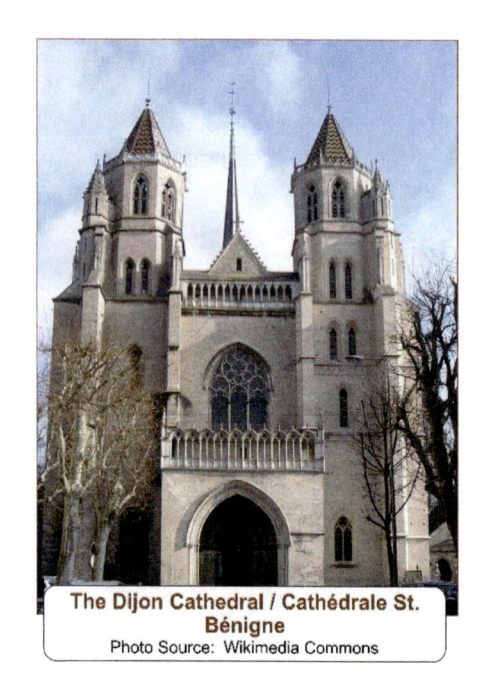

The Dijon Cathedral / Cathédrale St. Bénigne
Photo Source: Wikimedia Commons

tower collapsed which heavily damaged large sections of the church below.

Don't miss the **Roman-era crypt** under the Dijon Cathedral.
Photo source: Wikimedia

This is the largest church in Dijon but is not as ornate as the Church of Notre-Dame. View its expansive structure and plan on including a visit to the Roman-era crypt. There is a small fee to tour the crypt.

Where: The cathedral sits on the southern edge of the historic district and is an 8-minute walk southwest from the Place de la Libération.

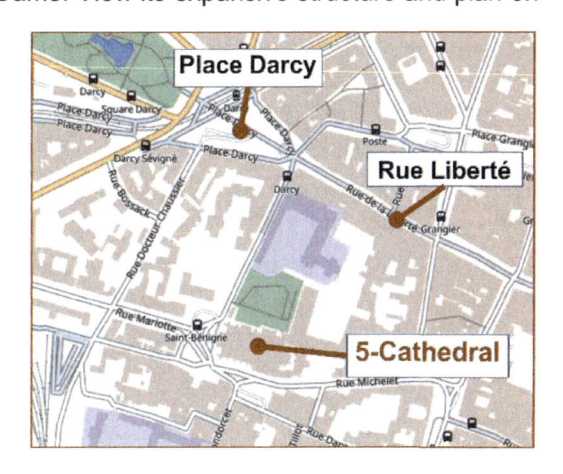

6-Magnin Museum / Musée Magnin: A collection of over 2,000 works of art which is housed in what had once been a prominent mansion near the center of Dijon.

Coming here, the visitor has the experience of not only viewing an impressive art collection, but also exploring an impressive townhouse. The mansion was built in the 17th century and later modified in 1930 by Maurice Magnin.

Magnin Musem
A 17th century mansion which is now a large gallery.

Over the years the Magnin family collected a large number of artworks. These works were given to the city in 1938 along with the conditions that the building retains the character of a private home and the collection would remain intact.

Where: The mansion is less than a block from Place de la Libération on Rue des Bons Enfants.

When Open: Closed on Monday. Open Tuesday to Sunday in the morning from 10am to 12:30. Closed for lunch and reopens at 1:30PM until 6PM.

Cost: No fee to view the permanent exhibits.

Website: www.Musee-Magnin.fr.

Dijon Points of Interest

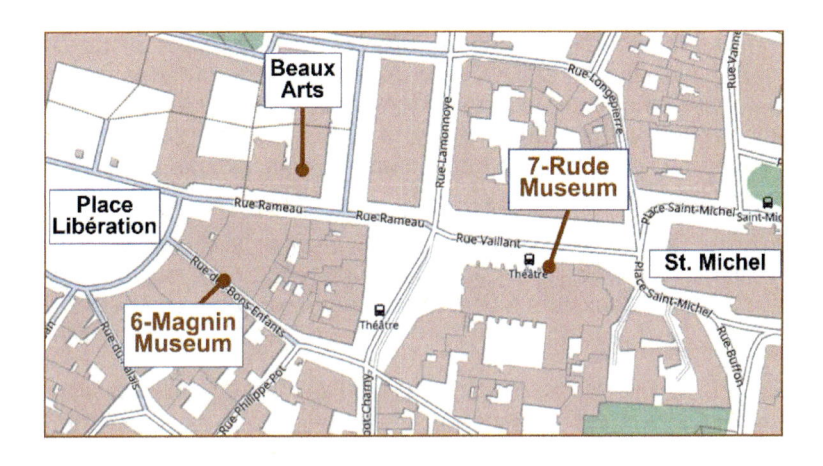

7-Rude Museum / Musée Rude: A museum which is dedicated to the works of the French Sculptor François Rude. Established in 1947 and placed inside Saint-Stephens church which sits near the Dukes Palace complex.

La Marseillaise
One of many impressive sculptures in Musée Rude.

The museum has numerous life-size plaster casts of major works done by the artist. The originals for many of these works are elsewhere such as the La Marseillaise which is incorporated into the Arc de Triomphe in Paris. In addition to the François Rude works, the museum also houses archeological works such as a crypt from the 11th century.

Where: The museum is inside Saint Stephen's church on Rue Vaillant. This building also houses the city library. It is one block east of the Beaux-Arts Museum and the Place de la Libération.

Cost: No entry fee.

When Open: Closed Tuesday and major holidays. Hours vary slightly depending on the season. Open times are generally from 10AM to 6PM.

Website: www.beaux-arts.dijon.fr. This website covers several museums including the Rude Museum, Beaux-Arts and others.

8-Burgundy Life Museum / Musée de la Vie Bourguignonne:
Established in a former monastery, this museum is devoted to life in Burgundy (Burgundian) as it was in the late 19th century. Collections are built around depicting how life was in this region including shopping, farming, and commerce.

Where: The museum is located inside the Bernardines Monastery situated an 8- to 10-minute walk south of the Place de la Libération. Trams do not service this location.

Museum of Burgundian Life has numerous life-size exhibits.

Cost: No charge to visit the permanent collections. There is a modest fee for guided tours.

When Open: Closed Tuesdays Open all other days except major holidays. Note: the opening hours are split with the museum open in the morning until 12:30 and then closed for lunch. It reopens at 2PM and then remains open until 6PM.

Facilities: Bookstore and restrooms. The museum does not include a restaurant. The nearest restaurants are one block west on Rue Berbisey.

Website: www.Musees.Dijon.fr This site covers several museums including this one.

9-Jardin Darcy (Darcy Park): Dijon's first park which was built over the town's reservoir. The main features here are the large water fountain, gazebo, and polar bear sculpture. The park, and neighboring plaza, were named after Henri Darcy, who was an early civil engineer for Dijon. He created the underground water works which greatly transformed the city. Due to his efforts, Dijon was one of the first cities in Euro pe to have a public water system and network.

This city park, which is slightly over 2 acres (1 hectare) in size was built in 1880 and is noted for its numerous statues and children's play areas. An interesting aspect of the park is the large underground reservoir which, until recently, had been used to supply drinking water to much of the city. This changed when the tram system was put in place and now the reservoir is largely used to store run-off water.

Jardin Darcy / Darcy Park

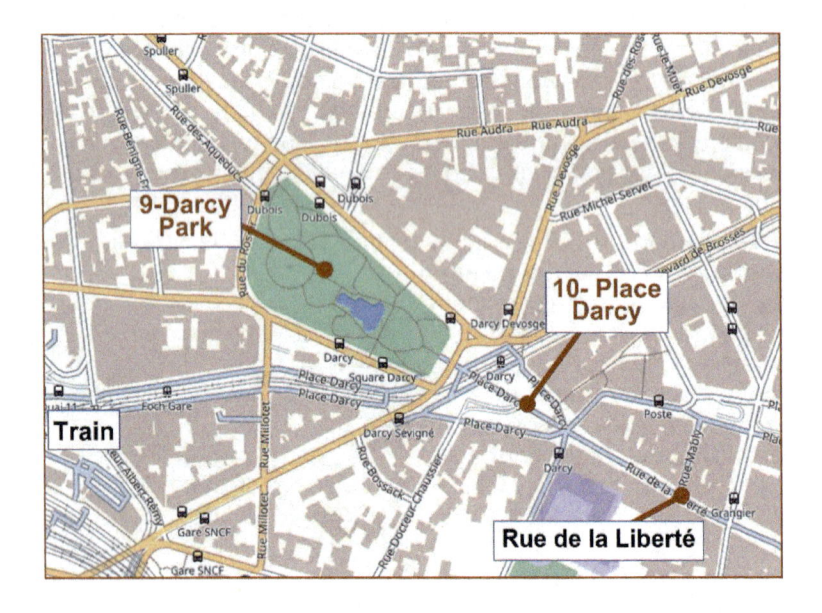

10- Place Darcy and William Gate: Place Darcy, or Darcy Square, is the spot where most first-time visitors begin their explorations of Dijon. It sits at the entrance to the pedestrian shopping street Rue de la Liberté, which then takes visitors into the heart of historic Dijon and Place de la Libération. It is also quite helpful that both of the city's tram lines stop here along with it being a short walk to the train station.

This busy plaza, which was rebuilt in the 1880's, has been known to exist since the Middle Ages. At that time, it had a fortified gate and defensive system. For travelers coming from Paris in the late 19th century, this was the main road leading into Dijon.

Darcy Square (Place Darcy)
Facing toward **William Gate** (Porte Guillaume)
Photo Source: Google Maps

Today, the earlier fortifications are mostly gone and there now stands a prominent city gate, the Guillaume Gate, or William Gate. It was built with the goal of giving the city a grand entrance. The name of the gate comes from Guillaume de Volpiano, an early abbot of Dijon's Saint Bénigne abbey.

Today, the plaza is bordered by Haussmann style buildings[11] which have several shops and restaurants. There is even a parking area underneath the plaza.

11-Rue de la Liberté: This is, by far, the most notable and popular pedestrian shopping street in Dijon. This lane stretches for 1/3 of a mile (1/2 km) with end points at Place Darcy and Place de la Libération. Along the route, there are numerous boutiques,

Shops along **Rue de la Liberté**.

---

[11] **Haussmann Style Buildings:** This is the architectural style which is very prominent throughout Paris. This style, created by Georges Haussmann was created under Napoleon III.

restaurants and even the department store, Galeries Lafayette. One of the leading mustard shops, Moutarde Maille Dijon is here as well.

12-Mustard (Moutarde) Boutiques:

Two popular mustard (moutarde) boutiques may be found in the historic center. The two stores are within a few minutes' walk of each other. In both cases, you will find an impressive array of gifts including mustard, vinegar, other gifts, and the ability to bottle your own. Mustard tastings are generally provided along with guidance on the history and making of differing mustard products.

Dijon Mustard is no longer grown and produced only in this area as it originally was. As of 2009, it is no longer produced within Dijon, but there is still a factor in the small nearby town of Chevigny-Saint-Sauveur.

La Boutique Maille
Popular Mustard/Moutarde shop in the historical district.

Currently about eighty percent of the mustard seeds used in local production come from Canada.

The Two Boutiques:

- La Maison Maille. Located at 32 Rue de la Liberté, roughly midway between William Gate and the Dukes Palace complex. www.Maille.com

- La Moutarderie Edmond Fallot: Located at 16, Rue de la Chouette. Tucked away on a quiet cobblestone street near the cathedral Église Notre-Dame. www.Fallot.com. They also have a factory which offers tours and a store in Beaune.

When Open: Normal hours for both stores are 10AM to 7PM, 7-days a week. Check the store's website for hours for when you will visit.

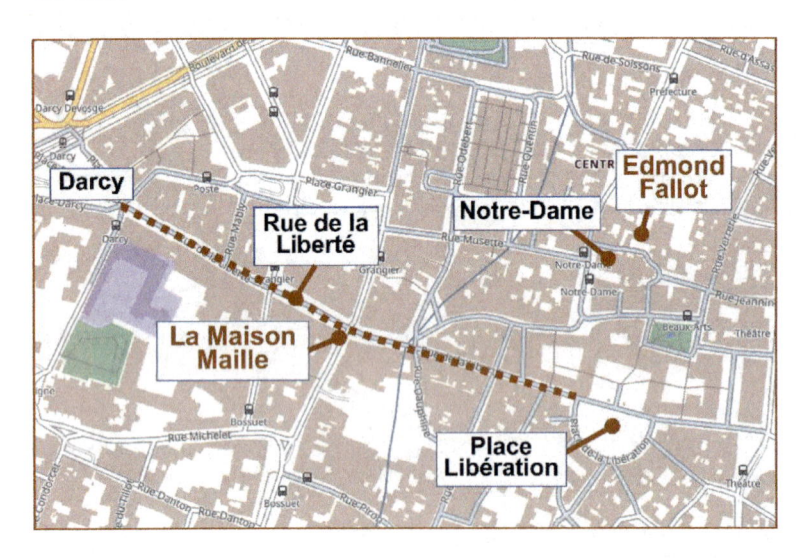

13-Les Halles Market:[12] Often referred to simply as "The Market" this is a large hub of activity for many who live in and near Dijon. This market is one of the best places to discover local produce, cheese, wine, meat, and more. If you are interested in the Burgundy region's cuisine and gourmet lifestyle, this lively market offers everything you want. You may also buy prepared meals here and sit and enjoy them while visiting.

A great place to explore the area's cuisine.
Les Halles Market

Les Halles is in a large cast-iron building which was built in the late 1800s and was modeled after a similar market in Paris.

Where: The market is in the historic center, a 6-minute walk north and west of the Place de la Libération. If you wish to reach it by tram, both lines T1 and T2 stop at "Godrans" which is a short walk north of the market.

When Open: The best days to visit are Tuesday, Friday, or Saturday. On these 3 days each week, all elements of the market

---

[12] **Les Halles Name:** The formal French name of this produce market is La Conciergerie des Halles.

inside and the vendors outside are open. If you visit on a Thursday, only the inside portions of the market are open. Closed on Monday, Wednesday, and Sunday.

Facilities: Eating areas and restrooms are available.

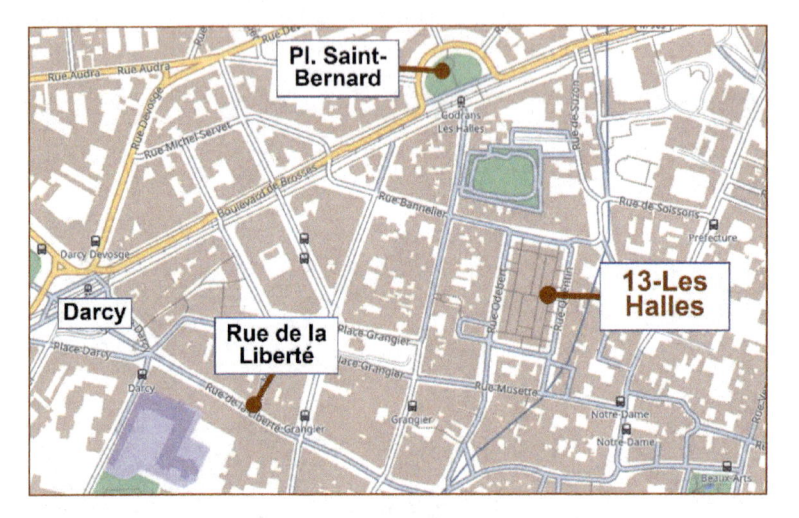

14-Botanical Park & Natural History Museum: A short walk south of the train station is a large park and museum complex which is easily reached on foot. The sites include:

Botanical Garden / Jarden Botanique de l'Arquebuse: This is a 12-acre (5 hectare) park, botanical garden and arboretum. The gardens are intended to be a showcase of over 4,000 species of plants. In addition to the formal gardens, there are ponds to explore and a children's play area. There is no cost to enter. The address is: 1Avenue Albert, 21000 Dijon. Often referred to simply as the Arquesbue Garden.

Natural History Museum / Muséum d'historie Naturelle: This modest museum sits along the northern side of the gardens and park. Located in what had once been a military barracks, the museum is a popular attraction for schools and families with a focus on biodiversity.

Planaterium: This is a large domed theater which presents digital shows of the solar system, the universe and other topics such as Darwin or dinosaurs. Details on offerings may be found within the city's website: www.Metropole-Dijon.fr.

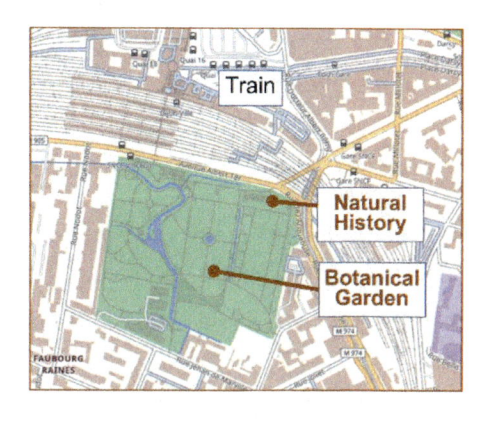

15-The International Cité of Gastronomy and Wine:
This food-and-wine oriented destination (Cité Internationale de la Gastronomie) is new to Dijon and the Burgundy region as it just opened in May 2022. A one-sentence description of this very large complex is difficult as there is a lot here, but it is not a tourist destination per se.

Do not come here as a typical tourist as you may be disappointed but **DO** come here if you have an interest in local food and wine and wish to

Cité Internationale de la Gastronomie

learn more. Some of what you will find here includes:
- Food oriented classes
- Gourmet boutiques
- Stores dedicated to food and wine, including a specialty bookstore.
- Specialty restaurants and a food court
- Burgundy wine school
- Baking, pastry and cooking classes
- Expositions and fairs geared to gastronomy

Location: This facility is slightly south of the train station and the above-cited botanical garden. The best way to travel here is by tram and there is a convenient station here, the "Monge-Cité de la Gastronomie" stop.

Website: www.CiteDeLaGastronomie-Dijon.fr

9: Beaune – Burgundy's Wine Capital

Located approximately 38km/23 miles southwest of Dijon is the historic town of Beaune which is thought by many to be the ***Wine Capital of Burgundy***.

This is a midsize town of nearly 22,000 people, located on the noted Burgundy Wine Trail (Route des Grands Crus). It is a compact and picturesque town filled with a maze of small, cobblestone streets, timber-framed houses, and filled with shops and restaurants.

This town is a gastronomical treasure for some as there are many specialty boutiques and restaurants offering some of the world's best wines, cheeses, and delicacies. Even for individuals who are not wine aficionados, visiting the wine caves (cellars) and sitting in on a wine class can be a lot of fun.

> **A Good Alternative to Staying in Dijon**
>
> If your primary goal is to explore Burgundy's vineyards, staying here may be a good option.

The focal point is the ***Hospices de Beaune,*** a hospital founded in the Middle Ages. The Gothic design with intricate and colorful tile roofs is unique and calls out for photographers to capture its beauty.

One caution, Beaune is a popular destination and can be crowded during the summer months. On the plus side, it is during this time that all tours, shops, and restaurants are open and operating.

A Starting-Point Guide

Traveling to Beaune from Dijon: Beaune is a short distance south of Dijon and easy to reach by car or train. There is no commercial airport here.

Train: Numerous trains depart from Dijon's main station (Gare de Dijon-Ville) every day. Depending on the train you select, travel time will be between 20 to 30 minutes each way.

Beaune's train station is a 10- to 15-minute walk into the heart of the town's historic area. Taxis may be available but are not always present as this is a small town. The walk into the center is along a pleasant tree-lined boulevard.

The town is circled by ancient ramparts and the walk from the train station takes you through one of the old gates with fortifications. At this point, the road narrows significantly as you will find yourself in the maze of cobblestone roads which define Beaune. Follow signs pointing to "Centre Ville" to reach the area with shops, attractions, and restaurants.

Buses from the train station are available and come by the train station frequently. A map of the town's bus routes is posted at the stop outside the train station to help you determine which bus to catch.

Car: If you are coming by car, the quickest route is a 35- to 40-minute drive from central Dijon to Beaune along a major highway, the A31.

An alternate route is to follow the Burgundy Wine Route along the D974. This way is slower (at least 20 minutes longer) but takes you through much of the Burgundy wine region. Once you are in Beaune, several car parks are near the Tourist Office, which is a great place to start exploring.

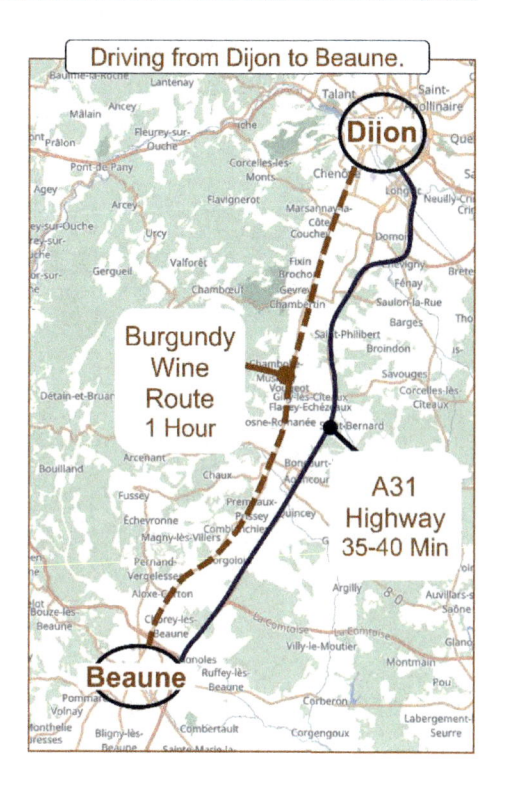

Driving from Dijon to Beaune.

Burgundy Wine Route 1 Hour

A31 Highway 35-40 Min

Beaune Apps

Several apps for the town of Beaune are available and most provide detailed maps and guidance to the leading attractions.

What to See and Do in Beaune:
The historic center of Beaune is the main attraction by itself. While there are a few notable attractions here, just walking around this charming town and exploring the narrow streets can be a delight and should be the primary goal of visiting here.

Tourist Office: Consider making this your first stop when you arrive in Beaune. Located a 15-minute walk from the train station, this office can provide detailed maps, information on local and area tours, winery guidance, and help on restaurants, hiking trails, and lodging.

The website for the Beaune Tourist Office is: www.Beaune-Tourism.com. Click on the section inn this site detailing the Tourist office.

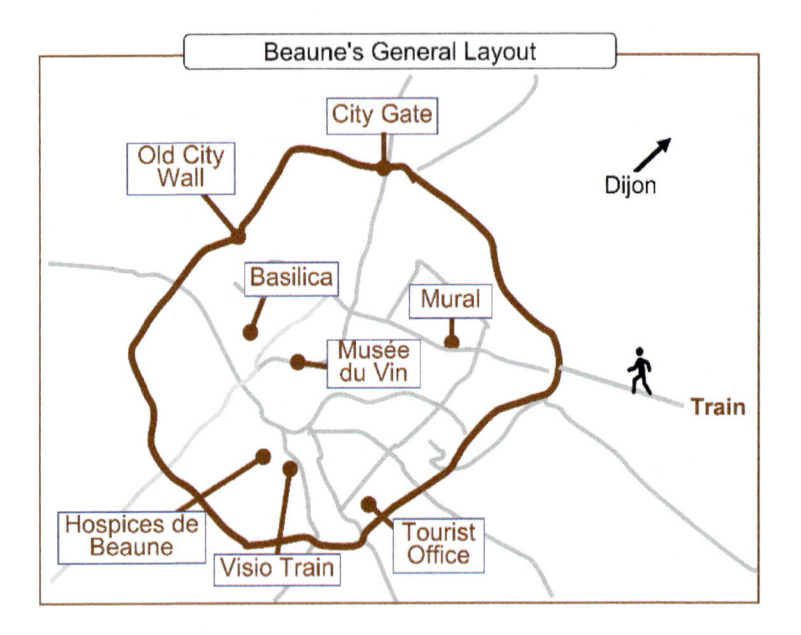

Beaune's General Layout

- City Gate
- Old City Wall
- Basilica
- Mural
- Musée du Vin
- Dijon
- Train
- Hospices de Beaune
- Visio Train
- Tourist Office

Hospices de Beaune: Also referred to as the Hôtel Dieu. This is Beaune's most iconic building due to it distinct 15th century Burgundian design. Built in 1443, it was created as a hospital for the poor. When founded, this was a time when the majority of the local population was poor due to wars and the plague. This small complex is arranged in two, two-story buildings, each with complex tile work on the rooftops and half-timbered sides.

This unique structure now serves multiple purposes including a museum. This building is where the annual wine auction is held. It is generally open to view the hospital interior and tall, vaulted wood ceilings.

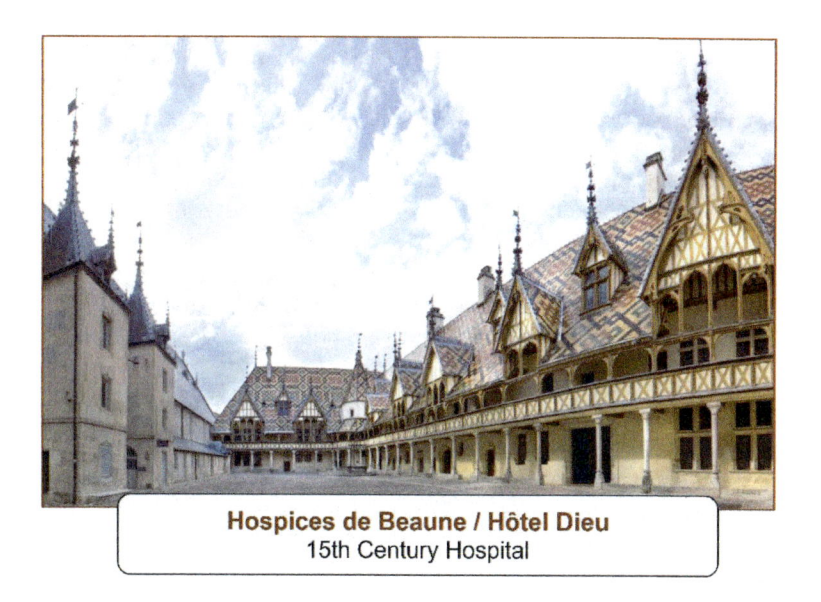

Hospices de Beaune / Hôtel Dieu
15th Century Hospital

Musée du Vin (Burgundy Wine Museum): This is the first museum in France exclusively devoted to wine. It is situated in the former mansion of Burgundy dukes and is in the heart of Beaune. Inside there is a large, permanent exhibition spread over two floors.

Come here to learn about the history of viticulture, practices, and the business of wine growing. Among the exhibits is an impressive collection of old wine presses. Many of the permanent exhibits were completely updated recently to provide a modern and interactive experience.

Hours: Closed Tuesday. All other days from 10AM to 6PM with a midday break.

Address: Hôtel des Ducs de Bourgogne, 24 rue Paradis. This building is close in style to the notable Hospices de Beaune.

~ ~ ~ ~ ~

Our Lady of Beaune Basilica: (Basilique Notre-Dame de Beaune) A Romanesque styled church built in the 12th century with later additions from the Gothic and Renaissance eras. This is not a large church, but it does have several notable features. Allow about an hour to fully admire all that this beautiful complex has to offer including the collection of 15th century tapestries and the open Cloister.

It is located in the center of the historical area. The church and cloister are open most days from 8AM to 7PM. To view the tapestries, check the website for current times as viewing times are limited.

Basilica Website: www.Paroisse-Beaune.org

Basilica Notre-Dame in Beaune

City Gate / Porte Saint-Nicholas: Along the northern border of Beaune's historic is a city gate which was built in 1770 and was part of the city walls when it was first opened. Up until 1844 there was a wooden gateway and drawbridge. The adjoining city walls and moat were mostly eliminated at that time

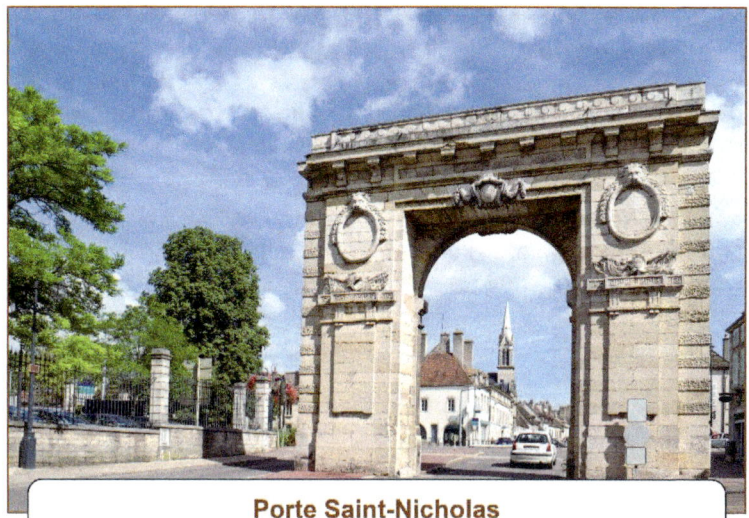

Porte Saint-Nicholas
An 18th century gate along the northern border of historic Beaune.

Visio Train / En Petit Train
A 40-minute narrated tour of Beaune and nearby vineyard.

Visio Train: A relaxed way to explore the historical area is to take the tourist train, officially referred to as the Visio Train or "***Le Petit Train***." This is a 40-minute narrated tour provided in the comfort of a train-like vehicle which tours the area highlights. This is not a "hop-on/hop-off" type of ride. Once you get on, riders are expected to stay on for the full circuit.

The largest pluses to this experience are: (a) narration which explains the highlights; (b) visit to several places which may otherwise be missed; and (c) the train takes riders out to a local vineyard.

Cost: Adults 10€ / Children 6€. (Subject to change)

Departure Point: In front of the Hospices de Beaune.

Seasonal: This ride only operates from April through October each year.

Website: www.VisioTrain.com

Cinema Mural: In the northeastern section of Beaune and tucked away in a small square, is the ***Mural de La Grande Vadrouille***. This cultural landmark was placed here in honor of a popular French movie filmed in Beaune in 1966. The movie, a comedy, was France's most popular for over 40 years.

Mural de la Grande Vadrouille

Staying in Beaune:[13] Beaune is a popular place to visit and the number of inns, B&Bs, and hotels attests to this. The volume of lodging opportunities is nearly that of Dijon, a much larger community.

If you are seeking to explore the area's wineries, Beaune's central location on the Burgundy Wine Route, along with the reduced traffic, makes this a good alternative to Dijon for lodging.

Most lodging here will be found in two general areas: (a) the compact historical area, and (b) the main road leading into town from the southeast. There are also some notable country estates and spas on the outskirts of town.

Lodging In Town: This is where to stay if you are coming here by train. Beaune's central area, primarily the area defined by the old city wall, provides a collection of small to mid-size boutique hotels. The nature of lodging here ranges from budget to upscale.

Suggested Lodging in Central Beaune		
Representative Sample Only – Not a Complete list of Beaune Lodging. (Lodging with 3 star or better rating)		
Hotel	**Address & Details**	**Rating**
Hôtel Athanor	9-11 Av. De la République Small, boutique property right in the heart of Beaune and convenient to shops and dining. www.Hotel-Athanor.com	3.5 stars
Hotel Le Cep	27 Rue Maufoux This is a premier, luxury property with full amenities and conference facilities. www.Hotel-Cep-Beaune.com	4.5 Stars

---

[13] **Hotel Ratings:** Ratings cited here are a composite of personal experience and popular lodging sites such as Trip Advisor and Booking.com

A Starting-Point Guide

Suggested Lodging in Central Beaune		
Representative Sample Only – Not a Complete list of Beaune Lodging. (Lodging with 3 star or better rating)		
Hotel	**Address & Details**	**Rating**
La Maison Blanche (The White House)	3 Rue Marey Upscale and contemporary. Modest size B & B. Check out the excellent wine cellar. www.LaMaison-Blanche.fr	4.5 stars
La Maison de Maurice	8 Rue Edouard Fraysse One of several top-quality boutique inns in Beaune. Large rooms and close to everything. Great wine bar. LaMaisonDeMaurice-Beaune.com	4.5 Stars
Maison Du Colombier	1 Rue Charles Cloutier An elegant, boutique inn in a classic building. Large rooms and a great restaurant. www.MaisonDuColombier.com	4 stars

Properties on the Road into Beaune: This option is only viable for individuals who are driving as this is not close walking distance to the train station and several properties are a bit outside of central Beaune. This main road enters town from the southeast.

This stretch offers the dual benefit of proximity to Beaune's historical center and ease of access to the highway to explore the area. The largest negative here is the overall lack of character and charm. There is little to offer to visitors here other than the row of mid-sized to large chain hotels.

Lodging on the main road into Beaune		
(All selected lodging has 3 star or better rating)		
Hotel	**Address & Details**	**Rating**
B&B Hotel Beaune Sud 1	1 Rue André Ampère Traditional roadside property. Good eating area. www.Hotel--bb.com	3.stars
Hôtel Kyriad Beaune	10 Rue Yves Bertrand Burgalat Nice atmosphere with great outdoor eating area, restaurant and wine bar. www.Beaune.Kyriad.com	3.5 Stars
Ibis Beaune La Ferme Aux Vins	Rue Yves Bertrand Burgalat Great outdoor pool to enjoy a summer day in. Good eating area and wine cellar. All.Accor.com	3.5 stars
Hôtel Mercure Beaune Centre	7 Av. Charles de Gaulle One of the best and larger hotels along this stretch. Comprehensive facilities including a large pool and good dining area. All.Accor.com	4.Stars
Novatel Beaune	25 Av. Charles de Gaulle Large hotel with good dining area, large grounds with pool and overall contemporary feel. Close to the highway. All.Accor.com	4 stars

10: Burgundy Vineyards & Wine Route[14]

The primary Burgundy (Bourgogne) wine region is not large, measuring 120km (about 75 miles) in length by 2km (1¼ miles) in width.[15]

Less than 5% of France's wines are produced here. Even with this modest size, the region offers some of the best-known and respected wines in the world. It is a complex area with thousands of small and mid-sized winemakers. In total, Burgundy wines cover about 70,000 acres of land. Most of this region is in one contiguous stretch south from Dijon. The one large exception is the Chablis growing area which is northwest from Dijon and has the beautiful small city of Auxerre at its center.

A key component for producing quality wine is the area's climate. Most of the Burgundy area (which excludes Chablis)

---

[14] **Minimal Wine Guidance Provided:** The purpose of this chapter is to supply a basic orientation to the nature of wines found near Dijon and the main Burgundy growing areas. **This is not an expert tutorial on Burgundy wine** as it is complex and would take much more than this brief chapter to detail.

[15] **Burgundy Wine Region:** The measurement of 120 x 2km does not include the Chablis area which sits apart from the main growing areas below Dijon.

has a climate with a mix of cold in the winter months to warm in the summer. Not surprisingly, the further south you go in this region, (in the direction of Lyon), the climate becomes warmer. This warm-to-cold cycle is a very important component of grape growth.

Burgundy Wine and Winery Resources

Want detailed information on Burgundy wines? Consider the following websites – each provides a wealth of details on area wines, wineries and available tours. You may also make wine tasting reservations on these sites:

www.WineFolly.com

www.WineTourism.com
Author favorite for booking tastings.

www.WineTraveler.com

Before providing guidance to tour this area, the following profile of this wine region may be helpful.

Burgundy Grape Varieties: There are primarily three grape varieties in the Burgundy region, Pinot Noir, Chardonnay and Gamay. Other, less prominent, grape varieties in the region include Sauvignon Blanc and Aligoté. In most cases, Burgundy wines are made from just one grape variety with blends being in the minority.

While the percentages of grapes grown varies by the area within Burgundy, the average across the region is:

- Chardonnay – 36% (This high percentage for a white grape comes as a surprise to most of us.)
- Gamay – 30%
- Pinot Noir – 30%
- The remaining 4% is spread across Sauvignon Blanc, Aligoté and others.

Some Helpful Wine Terminology:[16] The following terms are in common use across France and apply not only to Burgundy, but to most French wine regions. When touring the area's tasting rooms, the following terms are likely to arise and knowledge of them can be helpful.

Appellation: The specific area where a wine is grown. The wine must meet the specific guidelines for a locale. These guidelines are established by the "Appellation d' Origine Contrôlée (AOC). In Burgundy, there are 100 different appellations. These appellations are subdivided into the four quality categories of:

- Grand Cru
- Premier Cru
- Village
- Bourgogne (Burgundy Regional)

Terroir: (Pronounced Terr-wah). This is the foundation of the French wine AOC system which presumes that grapes impart unique qualities based on the specific habitat.

Terroir's components include: the nature of the soil, the elevation, is the area hilly or flat, the exposure to the sun, and the area's microclimate.

Grand Cru: The highest quality of wine which comes from a specific vineyard that maintains a consistent high quality with each vintage. To reach this quality, the wine must come from an exceptional growing site "Terroir." In Burgundy, there are 33 Grand Cru which produce around 2% (+/- 1%) of the wine in Burgundy.

- Côte de Nuits – 24 Grand Cru
- Côte de Beaune – 8 Grand Cru
- Chablis – 1 Grand Cru.

---

[16] **Wine App:** Many excellent apps are available to help you understand wine basics including the terminology and differences in wine growing areas. **"Wine Dictionary"** is the author's favorite.

Burgundy Wines By Quality Ranking

GRAND CRU
1 to 2% of Production

PREMIER CRU
11% of Production

VILLAGE Appellations
37% of Production

REGIONAL Appellations
50% of Production

NOTE: The percent of production cited varies based on the reference source used. Use this data as an approximation of the overall volume of wine in Burgundy for each quality level.

Premier Cru: First growth wines. High quality wines which are one step below Grand Cru. As with Grand Cru, these are vineyard-specific designations. In Burgundy, there are 630 +/- vineyards with this designation and account for 10 to 15% of wine production. The percentage and number of vineyards varies based on which reporting site is used.

Village Appellation Wine: As the name implies, these wines are specific to a community. They are considered higher quality than regional wines. Look for names like Santenay or Givry. There are 44 appellations in this category, and they account for nearly 40% of Burgundy wine production. The quality and price of these wines range substantially.

Regional Appellation Wines: These wines are the most frequently produced in Burgundy. A regional wine is not limited to a specific village and is typically a blend of grapes from multiple area villages. Village wines are commonly placed into subgroups such as:

- Bourgogne Rouge – Burgundy red
- Bourgogne Blanc – Burgundy white
- Bourgogne Rose – Burgundy rose'
- Crément de Bourgogne - Burgundy sparkling wine

Burgundy Wine Areas:[17] There are five geographically distinct Burgundy wine growing areas. Four of these wine areas are adjacent and run from north near Dijon, and south for roughly 75 miles to the town of Mâcon. The fifth wine area, Chablis, sits off by itself northwest of Dijon. The five recognized areas (from north to south) are: Chablis, Côte de Nuits, Côte de Beaune, Côte Chalonnaise and Mâconnaise. Descriptions of the five wine areas and listings of some wineries to explore follow.

Hundreds of vineyards small and large populate this area. Most of them do not have tasting rooms for individuals to simply drop in. Some only allow groups with advanced reservations. The good news is there are quite a few wineries, mostly larger, which accommodate visitors for tastings. Currently, it is best to check each winery's website prior to planning a visit.

In addition to visiting the wineries directly, several tasting rooms may be found in Dijon, Beaune, and the larger villages. These tasting rooms sell wines and provide tastings for Burgundy vineyards which often do not encourage direct on-site visits.

---

[17] **Specific Winery Guidance**: This edition of this guide does not detail specific wineries to visit. There are, to put it simply, too many and the rules for visiting them can and do change such as requiring advance reservations or not. If you are not taking a tour to visit area wineries (tours are strongly advised) consider using the apps outlined here to help determine which wineries best fit your preferences..

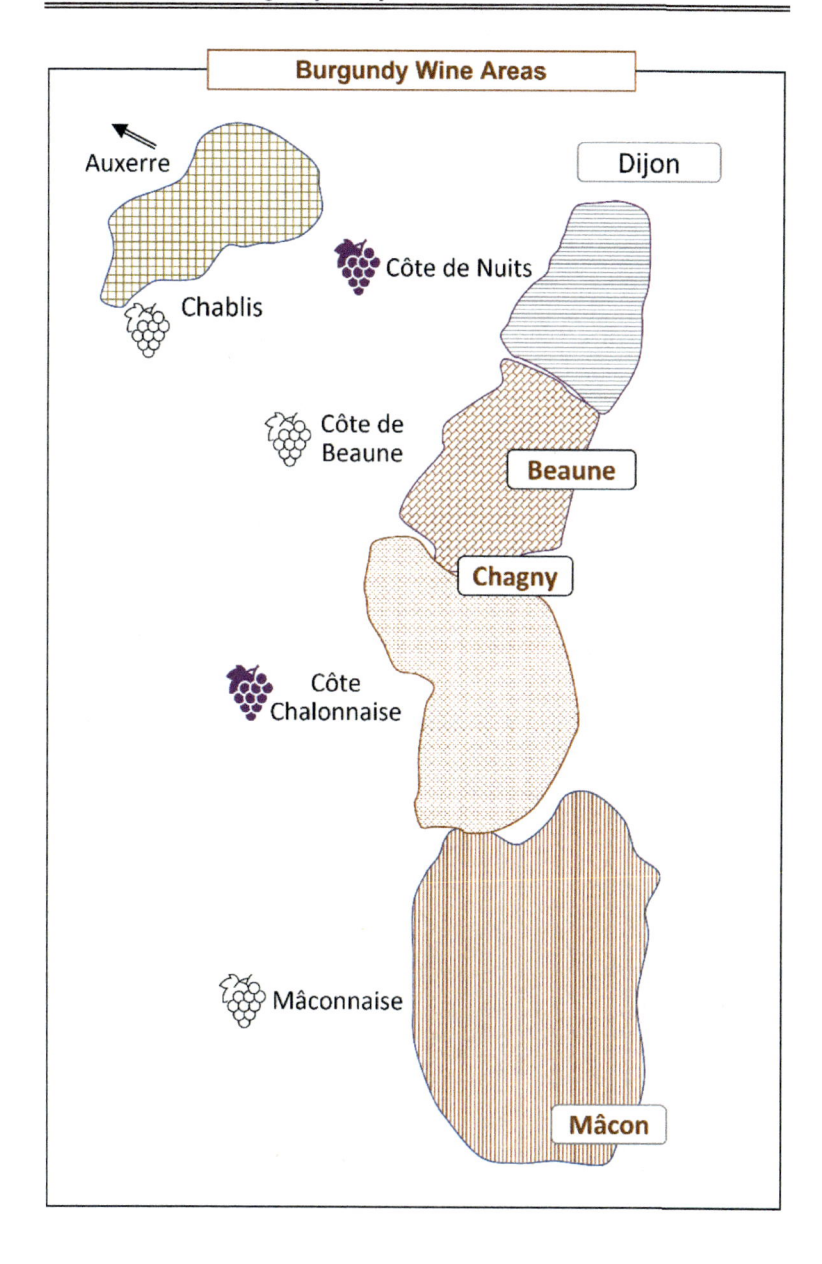

Burgundy Vineyards and Wine Route

Burgundy Wine Areas

Auxerre

Dijon

Côte de Nuits

Chablis

Côte de Beaune

Beaune

Chagny

Côte Chalonnaise

Mâconnaise

Mâcon

Côte de Nuits (The Night Slope): Closest to Dijon. The area is best for Pinot Noir. A majority of Burgundy's Grand Crus, 24 of them, are found in this small area. Wines here are some of the finest and most expensive in Burgundy if not the entire world.

This section of Burgundy is small and most of the vintners produce under 1,000 cases of wine each year. (In comparison, leading Bordeaux vineyards produce more than 20,000 cases per year)

Côte de Beaune (The Slope of Beaune): The popular town of Beaune is located here. Chardonnay is the leading wine here with eight Grand Cru vineyards. Seven of the Grand Cru vineyards produce whites, mostly Chardonnay. Wines here range from moderate to high in price.

Côte Chalonnaise (The Chalon slope): Located south of Beaune. Pinot Noir and sparkling Crémant are the leading wines here. This area does not have any Grand Cru vineyards. The area's rolling hills are dotted with many small, attractive villages which can offer a delightful road trip.

Château de Rully (Rully Castle)
12th century castle and winery in the Côte Chalonaise wine region of Burgundy.

Mâconnais (The region of Mâcon): The southern-most of the five Burgundy wine areas, it is best known for its Chardonnay. Wines here tend to be more affordable. The climate, due to Mediterranean influence, is slightly warmer than the rest of Burgundy, giving it a longer growing period.

Chablis: A separate wine section not in line with the other four. Chablis is located west and a bit north of Dijon. The climate here differs from the rest of Burgundy with colder winters and hotter summers. Also, the soil is different as much of it is limestone. There is one Grand Cru in Chablis and all wines made here are white. Most of the wines are made with Chardonnay grapes.

Burgundy Wine Route – the "Route des Grands Crus":

A popular and enjoyable way to experience the best of Burgundy's wine is to travel the *Burgundy Wine Route*. Following this route takes you through the two northern wine areas of Côte de Nuits and Côte de Beaune.[18]

The route extends from Dijon's southern edge south to the town of Santenay below Beaune. Depending on your starting point, the total journey is roughly 60km (37 miles). Along the way, there are dozens of attractive villages in addition to some of the world's most noted wines.

---

[18] **Côte de Or (Golden Slope):** The name often used to describe the combined area of Côte de Nuits and Côte de Beaune.

A Starting-Point Guide

Route des Grands Crus

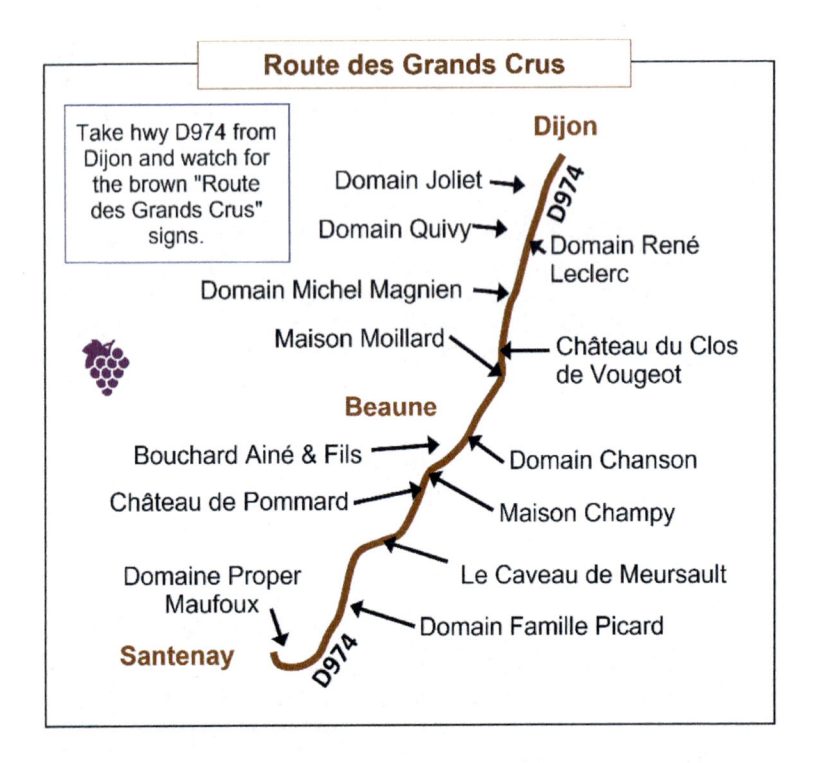

Take hwy D974 from Dijon and watch for the brown "Route des Grands Crus" signs.

Dijon
- Domain Joliet
- Domain Quivy
- Domain René Leclerc
- Domain Michel Magnien
- Maison Moillard
- Château du Clos de Vougeot

Beaune
- Bouchard Aîné & Fils
- Domain Chanson
- Château de Pommard
- Maison Champy
- Le Caveau de Meursault
- Domaine Proper Maufoux
- Domain Famille Picard

Santenay

It is important to note that this road only covers a portion of Burgundy's wine area. While the focus here is on the Grand Crus, when traveling this route, you will have the opportunity to taste wines in all classes ranging from regional to Grand Cru.

Trains are not a viable way to experience this area. Renting a car or joining one of the many tours departing from Dijon will be necessary.

Burgundy Wine Tours: Several tours are available out of Dijon and Beaune. The tours are more expensive than doing this on your own but there are two significant benefits:

> **Trip Advisor** is an excellent place to start when looking for available wine tours.
>
> In addition, when in Dijon, the Tourist Office has several area wine tours available.

- Many wineries only accept group tours with advanced reservations. Individuals trying to visit some of the more noted vintners will be unable to do so.
- Tours will provide knowledge of the area which can be valuable. Along with this, many wine tours will take their groups to locales which the casual visitor could miss.

Numerous companies offer these tours, and they range from half-day to multi-day itineraries. A sample of these services follows.

- **Burgundy Discovery:** As the name implies, this tour company is local to Dijon and the Burgundy region. They offer several private and small-group tours, primarily out of Beaune. Most tours are immersive full day tours. www.BurgundyDiscovery.com

- **Authentica Tours:** Private and small group wine tours departing out of Dijon and Beaune. A private tour will range between 500 to 1,000 Euro. Tours conducted by English-speaking guides with wine expertise. www.Authentica-Tours.com.

- **Into The Vineyard Tours**: Week-long, in-depth tours geared to small groups who wish to do a deep dive into Burgundy wine and cuisine. Can be customized to fit specific preferences. Expensive but well-rated. www.IntoTheVineyard.com.

- **Viator:** A subsidiary of Trip Advisor. A great service to find wine tours out of Dijon or Beaune. Group and private tours available, ranging from low-cost to expensive. www.Viator.com – then search for Burgundy wine tour.

- **Get Your Guide:** Similar to Viator in offerings and price range. They resell a large variety of tours, including wine tours out of Dijon and Beaune. www.GetYourGuide.com – then search for Burgundy wine tour.

- **Beaune France Tourist Office**: Beaune is considered to be the heart of the Burgundy wine district, and they offer numerous tours of the local area. A favorite of many are their bike tours of area vineyards. Check the tours section at www.Beaune-Tourism.com.

11: Burgundy by Boat & Bicycle

Several enjoyable alternatives for how to explore Dijon and Burgundy are available. In addition to traditional tours, wine tastings and general area explorations, consider partaking in one of the several outdoor means of touring the area.

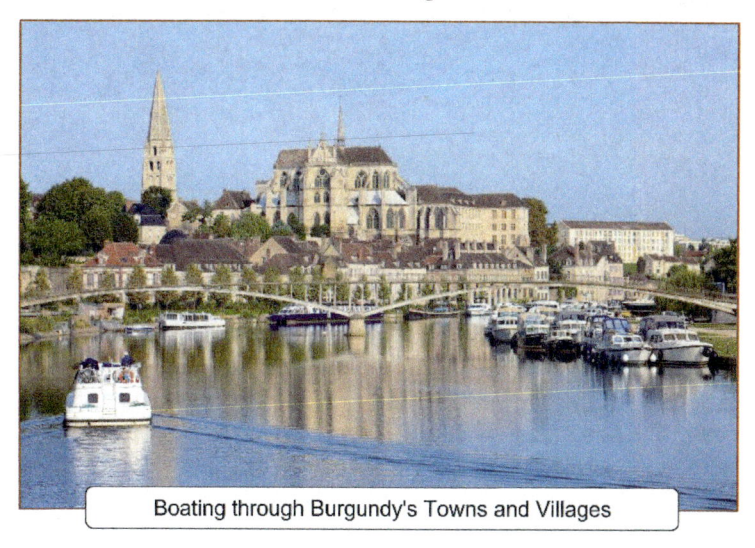

Boating through Burgundy's Towns and Villages

It is easy to think of Burgundy as primarily an area to explore wine and villages and this is a correct assumption. However, immersing yourself in the area's natural and outdoor opportunities can greatly enhance a visit to this area.

The following are several opportunities for touring the area which, depending on your abilities, can add a lot of fun.

Information in this chapter provides guidance on two of the leading ways to explore the region: by boat and by bicycle.

Boat Rentals and Boat Tours: Most of the Burgundy area boat excursions are several days in length. A limited number of partial day or dinner boat trips are available and most of these depart near Auxerre in the Chablis district.

Cruising Burgundy's Canals
Consider taking a self-drive boating tour of Burgundy's rivers and

Boating along the waterways of Burgundy is a great way to experience the area from a different and much slower point of view. Often, the boats are equipped with motorized bikes for ease of exploring the villages and countryside along the route.

Some boat trips start out of the small Port de Dijon, in the southern section of the city and easy to reach by Dijon's tram system. Most boating trips, especially barge and boat rentals, will depart from either the waterfront in the town of Auxerre or the large Marina St-Jean-De-Losne in the town of Saint-Usage, a 40-minute drive from central Dijon.

Burgundy Navigable Waterways

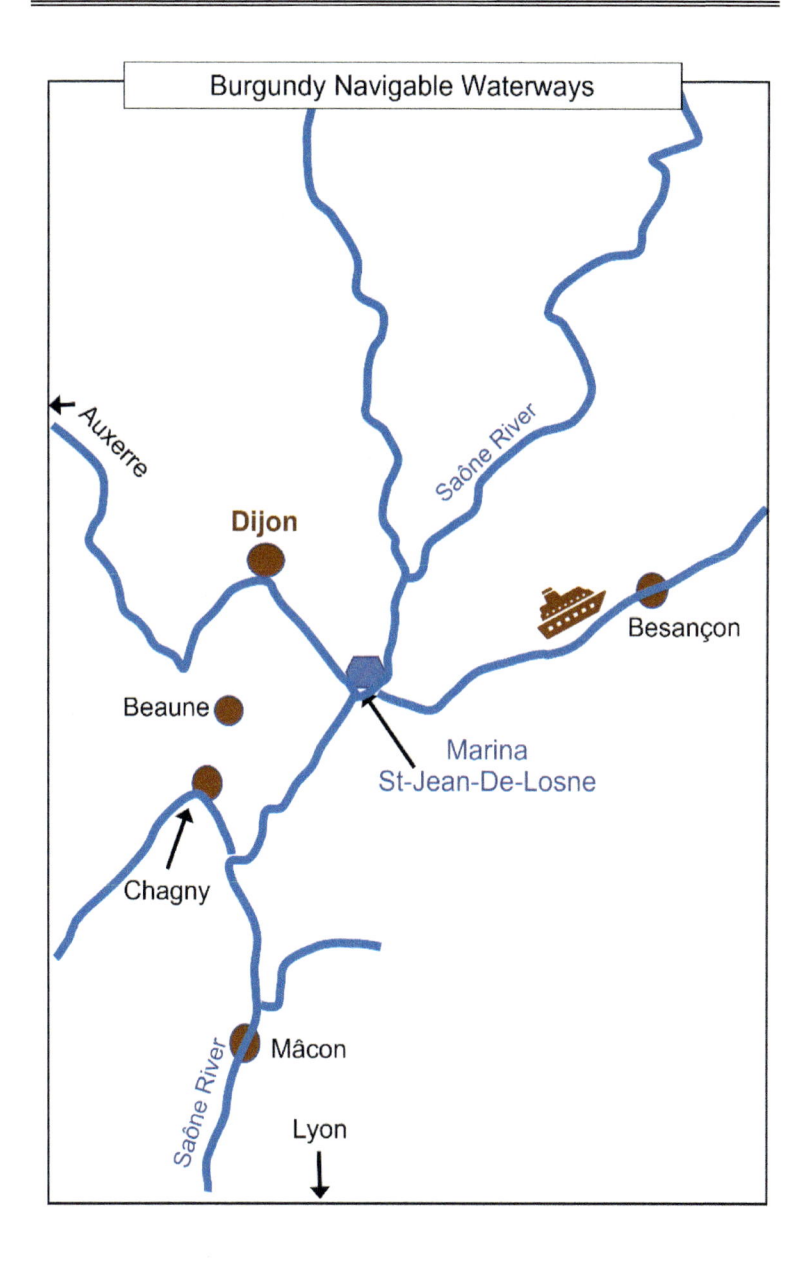

- Auxerre
- Dijon
- Besançon
- Beaune
- Marina St-Jean-De-Losne
- Chagny
- Mâcon
- Lyon

Saône River

103

A Starting-Point Guide

> **Burgundy Boat Tour and Rental Resource**
>
> See Burgundy-Canal.com for a listing of boat rental companies and hotel barges.

Two main types of Burgundy trips are available: (a) self-drive and (b) chartered or small-hotel barges with a qualified captain and staff.

The self-drive boats offer advantages of going at your own pace and the price is much less than a boat with captain and staff. Some learning is necessary to pilot these boats. A leader in European canal boat rentals is leBoat.com. The staff will instruct you on the basics of boat handling and how to navigate the locks.

Burgundy Bicycle Rental & Tours: Bicycling through wine country can be a joy, even for those who are not athletes, thanks to the popular Ebikes. Chapter 6 cited *Divia Mobilities* which enables riders to pick up and drop off bicycles at numerous stations

Explore Burgundy by Bicycle
Many bike tours from Dijon and Beaune are available.

> **Consider Renting an E-Bike**
>
> Most bicycle rental firms will provide the option of renting an electric bike. Ebikes dramatically reduce the effort required to tour the area.

throughout Dijon. In addition to this, several companies throughout the region allow for bike rentals ranging from hourly rates to weekly.

Most bicycle rental companies in Burgundy are based in Dijon or Beaune. Some will bring bicycles directly to your hotel.

There are roughly 2,900 kilometers (1,800 miles) of bicycle trails throughout the greater Burgundy region. This vast network of trails allows you to design an itinerary which fits your preferences.

Types of Bicycle Routes: The trails can be put into three broad classifications: wine routes, canal routes or natural parks.

Wine Routes: Bike trails south of Dijon, along the Burgundy route. The routes range from level to low hills and visit numerous villages and wineries. Beaune is one of the most popular starting points for these trails as there is a good variety of topography, wineries, and distances for a ride. It is easy to have a circular ride with little or no overlap in the area covered.

Canal Routes: Bike along Dijon's major canal, the Burgundy Canal or "Canal de Bourgogne." These are completely level rides with the trail always alongside the canal. Most rides start out of Dijon head either west or southeast, depending on your preference. Most portions of these routes are rural. Most trips are out-and-back, causing the rider to reach a desired end point and then do the same trail for the return leg.

Natural Park: An hour drive west of Dijon is a huge park, the Morvan Regional Natural Park or "Parc Naturel Régional du Morvan." This is an excellent area for cycling in nature. Topography is gentle rolling hills, and the trails are mostly in natural settings. Many small villages dot this area adding to the fun. The number of bicycle rental companies servicing this area is far fewer than those which provide bicycle rentals along the wine trails.

Bicycle Rental Companies in Burgundy: Several companies in Burgundy provide both bicycle rental and bicycle tours. The following are sample listings of some of the leading firms by location.

	Burgundy Region Bike Rental and Tour Companies
Burgundy Bike	• Bike rentals and tours • Dijon and Nuits Saint-Georges • www.BurgundyBike.com
Cycle Classic Tours	• Bike rentals • Dijon, Beaune, & Chalon-sur-Saône • www.cctbikerental.com
Bourgogne Evasion	• Bike rentals and tours • Dijon and Beaune • www.BurgundyBikeTour.com
Divia Mobilities	• Bike rental • Dijon • www.Divia.fr

12: Nearby Towns to Explore
Day Trips Easily Done by Train

Exploring the villages and towns around Dijon is fun and can provide a great opportunity to experience portions of France which are not tourist oriented. These towns offer insights into normal life in France.

This guide does not list every place you could visit near Dijon or Beaune. The focus here is on a selection of "reachable" and delightful destinations by train or bus and on trips which can be done in one day without wearing yourself down.

Check out the graph on the following page for likely travel times to select towns from Dijon. This map only lists a few of the many locations which can easily be traveled to by train. These towns meet the criteria of:

> Each of the trips listed here may be done by taking a train or bus.
>
> Car rental is not needed for these trips.

- It takes less than 90 minutes each way by train or bus from Dijon.
- The town offers interesting sights and provides pleasant strolling.
- The town can easily be explored from the train station on foot or a convenient local transportation system.

Five towns are described in this chapter. There are many other wonderful villages and small towns which may also be visited. They are not included here if they do not meet the primary criteria of allowing for easy and pleasant access by local transportation.

A Starting-Point Guide

Day Trips by Train or Bus from Dijon

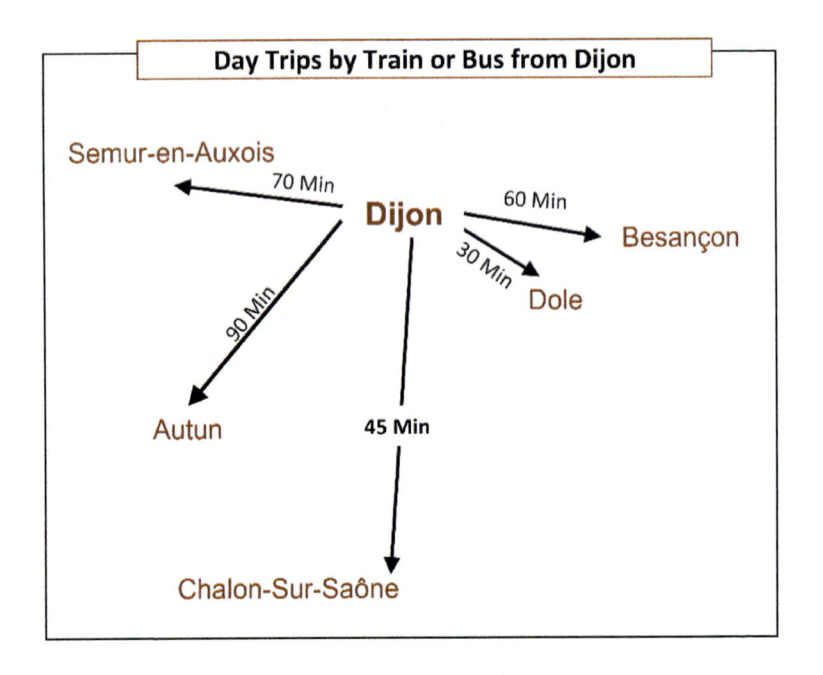

- Semur-en-Auxois — 70 Min
- Dijon
- Besançon — 60 Min
- Dole — 30 Min
- Autun — 90 Min
- Chalon-Sur-Saône — 45 Min

Suggested Burgundy Area Towns for Day Trips from Dijon
(Beaune is described in a separate chapter)

Town	Population	Travel Time from Dijon
Autun	15,000	90 minutes - Bus
Besançon	117,000	1 hour - Train
Chalon-sur-Saône	45,000	45 minutes - Train
Dole	24,000	30 minutes - Train
Semur-en-Auxois	4,200	70+ minutes - Bus

Autun: Located slightly southwest of Beaune, Autun is a historical treasure trove and an easy, relaxing, town to explore on foot. It was an early Roman town which once had as many as 100,000 people. Now the town is home to 15,000 people. Visitors will find several pleasant tree-lined streets, restaurants, and small parks to stroll in.

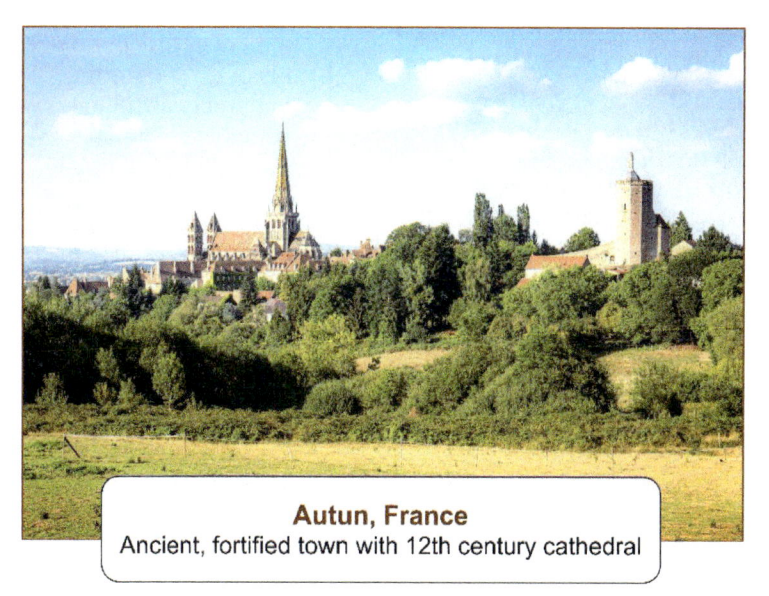

Autun, France
Ancient, fortified town with 12th century cathedral

Notable Autun Sights: The Roman influence is obvious in Autun and several ruins date back to the time of Augustus. Most of Autun's sights are within a 15-to-20-minute walk from the train/bus station. Among the many treasures are:

- **Autun Cathedral:** The Cathedral of Saint Lazarus of Autun. A 12th century Roman Catholic cathedral with Romanesque art and sculptures.

- **Roman Theater:** One of the largest in the western area of the Roman empire with 17,000 capacity. This is a pleasant 20-minute walk from the train station.

- **Two Roman Gates:** Porte Saint-André and Porte d'Arroux. Both are easy to reach on foot while exploring Autun.

- **Temple of Janus:** Located outside of the town centre. Built in Neolithic times.

- **City Wall:** Dating to the 1st century AD, there are 4 kilometers (over 2 miles) of restored ancient ramparts including several turrets.

Traveling to Autun: The trip from Dijon is roughly 90 minutes each way. The most frequent mode of travel is the area's excellent bus system. Train/bus combinations do depart Dijon for Autun, but the number of daily trips is limited.

> **Semur-en-Auxois**
>
> Another option, which is similar to Autun, is the quaint town of Semur-en-Auxois. It is a bit over an hour by bus or driving from Dijon and is absolutely stunning. The only downside is that traveling to here is a more of a challenge than the other towns cited in this chapter

Trains and buses depart Dijon at the Gare Ville (Dijon's major train station) and arrive at Gare Autun. Once at the station, the town's commercial center starts just one block away.

Autun Website: The tourist office's website which provides full details on the town is: www.Autun-Tourisme.com

Besançon: This is the largest and most active of the towns in this list. Located near the Swiss border, Bescançon has a dramatic and beautiful appearance with the Daubs River working around a sharp bend bordered by steep cliffs. The cliffs overlooking the river are dotted with numerous fortifications.

Besançon has several accolades includes being noted both as "The greenest city in France and a "Town of Art and History." The town's fortifications have been listed as a UNESCO World Heritage Site. There is a lot to see here, so allow a full day when traveling from Dijon. Consider spending a night or two here as

well as the number of historical sights easily rival Dijon and many other small cities of this size.

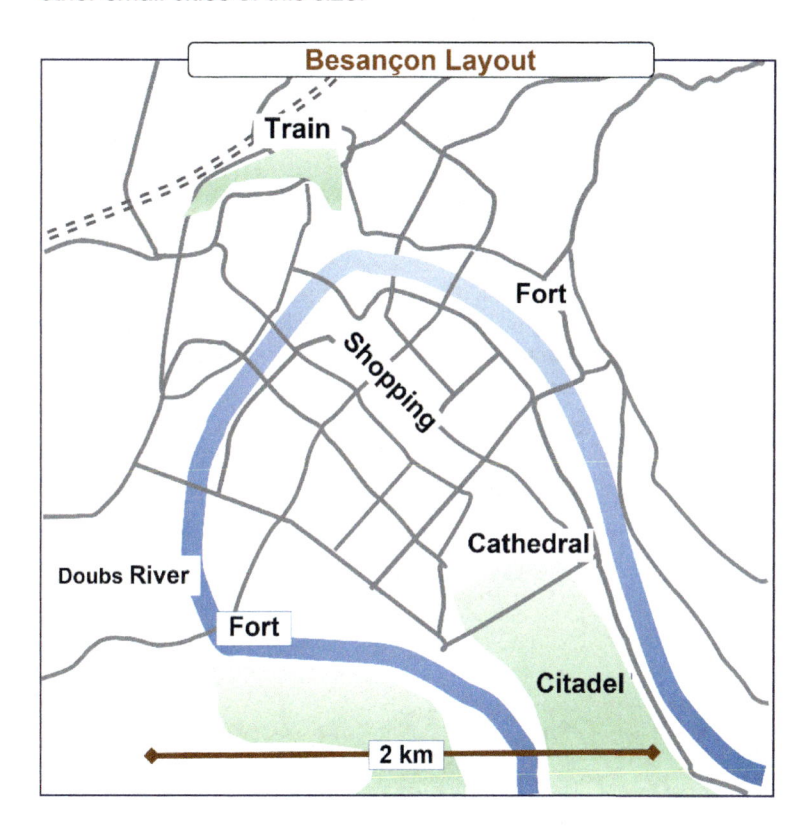

Besançon Layout

(Map showing: Train, Fort, Shopping, Doubs River, Fort, Cathedral, Citadel, 2 km scale)

Notable Besançon Sights: The central area of Besançon is circled on three sides by the River Daubs. The city has one of the best-preserved historic centers of any small city in France.

- **Revolution Square:** A large plaza at the foot of the town, near the river. A large fountain is in the center of the square and the popular pedestrian shopping street starts here.

- **Pedestrian Shopping Street:** The Rue des Granges is a 1-km street running through the center of the historic district. Some sections are limited to pedestrians, and it is lined with many shops and restaurants. Follow this street to the base of the hill where the Citadel is located.

- **Citadel** "Citadel de Besançon": Perched above the city, this large 29-acre complex provides a wealth of history to explore. Built in the 17th century, it is one of the most beautiful fortresses in France. Guided tours are available.

> The **"Little Train of Besançon"** takes riders to most of the major historic spots for a 45-minute tour.

- **Besançon Cathedral and Astronomical Clock:** A Roman Catholic church built in the 11th century. This large church is located in the historic district. The astronomical clock is one of the leading attractions in this complex.
- **Fortifications and Towers:** Besançon has several historical fortifications including towers (Tours). In most cases, these are situated on promontories overlooking the Doubs River.

Relax along the **Doubs River** in Bescançon

Traveling to Besançon: Trains are recommended from Dijon. The trip is roughly 1 hour each way depending on which train is taken. Take the train to the Gare de Besançon-Viotte station. This can be a bit confusing as most train trips will require a change in a station with a similar name – the "Gare Besançon-France-

Comté" station. This other station is outside of town and not convenient to visiting Besançon but changing trains here is easy and often needed.

Once you are at Besançon's station, look for the tram which is immediately outside. Take the tram to the "Révolution" stop and begin your explorations from there. If you choose to walk into town from the train station, it is a 20-minute walk to reach the historical center.

Besançon Website: www.Besancon-Tourisme.com.

Chalon-sur-Saône: As the town's name implies, this attractive small city of 45,000 is located on the Saône River. It is also in the heart of Burgundy wine country, a short distance south of Beaune.

Chalon-sur-Saône is best known as the birthplace of Photography. This history is recognized with a museum dedicated to

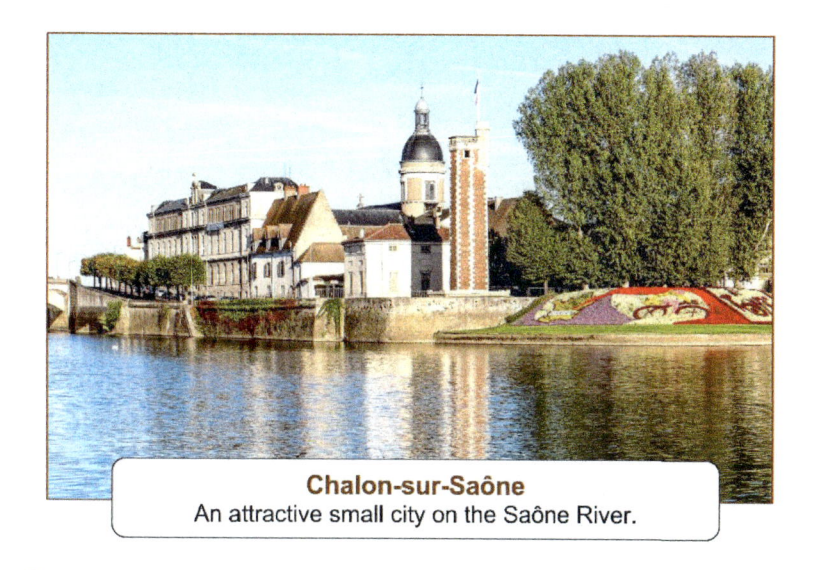

Chalon-sur-Saône
An attractive small city on the Saône River.

early photography including two-million photographs and numerous artifacts.

The historical center and riverfront are enjoyable areas to explore on foot. The number of river boats which make this a stop attests to this. Don't come here for major historical sites as they are limited. Come here for a small-city experience with minimal tourism.

For most individuals, a few hours in town will cover the bases. More time will be needed if you wish to use this as a springboard to the wineries in the area. Several tasting rooms (Caves) may be found in town where local wines may be sampled and purchased.

Traveling to Chalon-sur-Saône from Dijon: Trains are recommended from Dijon or Beaune. Travel time is around 45-minutes each way from Dijon. When arriving at the train station in Chalon-sur-Saône, it is a 15-to-20-minute walk to the oldest, more notable areas of town. Taxis are often available. Consider taking a taxi out to Cathédrale Saint-Vincent, which is situated at the far end of the historical area. From there, take an enjoyable walk back to the train station as you explore the town, restaurants, wine shops, and museums.

City Website: www.Achalon.com

Nearby Towns to Explore

Dole: This is the closest to Dijon of the towns outlined here. Similar to Salon-sur-Saône, this is a town to visit to get away from the tourist crowds and just enjoy the many history-laden, quiet streets. The Doubs River and Canal du Rhône run along the town's southeastern edge providing many attractive views.

The town of Dole and rental boats on the Canal du Rhône.

Dole is a photographer's delight. The old town and canals present many wonderful photo opportunities.

The historical center "Vieux Dole" is a medieval section of town full of winding streets, flower-lined canal, Roman road, and the home of Louis Pasteur.

A highlight when visiting here is the Fountain of the Lepers of Dole ("La Fontaine aux Lépreux"). This is an ancient bathhouse located in a hidden underground passage. Another popular attraction, especially for locals, is the active public market which is a hub of activity. This market is located outside large church "Collégiale Notre-Dame de Dole."

Traveling to Dole from Dijon: Trains are recommended from Dijon to Dole. Travel time is around 30 minutes each way from Dijon and no change of trains is required. Several trains depart each day. When arriving at the train station in Dole, it is a 10- to 15-minute walk to the historical area. Taxis are not frequent, but the town does have a local bus service which departs from the Dole train station, "Gare de Dole."

Appendix: Helpful Online References

To help you expand your knowledge of this area, several online reference sites are listed here. Dijon and the neighboring towns such as Beaune and the expansive Burgundy wine country are popular places to visit, so there is a wealth of materials which can help in planning your trip.

The following is a list of online references for this city and the area. The purpose of this list is to enhance your understanding before embarking on your trip. Any online search will result in the websites outlined here plus many others. These are listed as they are professionally done and do not only try to sell you tours.

1-Dijon and Burgundy Area Websites.	
Website Name	**Website Address and Description**
About France	www.About-France.com – then search for Burgundy. Overview of the Burgundy region, history, villages, wine tasting, and top attractions throughout the area.
Beaune Tourism	www.Beaune-Tourism.com Details on the town of Beaune, hotels, activities, wine tours.
Burgundy Tourism	www.Burgundy-Tourism.com Listings of events in Burgundy and Dijon, attractions, tours, local transportation, and information on Burgundy's towns and villages.

1-Dijon and Burgundy Area Websites.

Website Name	Website Address and Description
Culture Trip	www.TheCultureTrip.com – then search for Dijon. Overview of highlights of the city and area including restaurants, shopping, and museums.
Destination Dijon	en.DestinationDijon.com Website of Dijon's office of Tourism, providing details on the Owl's Trail, city pass, available tours, and activities.
Dijon Beaux Arts Museum	www.Beaux-Arts.dijon.fr. The main fine arts museum in Dijon.
Divia Mobilities	Divia.fr Use this site for detailed information on Dijon's transportation system and bicycle rentals.
Explore France	us.France.fr – then search for Dijon Highlights of the city's history, main sites, and fun things to do in Dijon including history of Dijon mustard.
Information on France	www.InformationOnFrance.com – then search for Dijon. Good details on the Dijon City Pass and what is included.
Magnin Museum	www.Musee-Magnin.fr Details on Dijon's popular Magnin Museum (art museum)
Trip Advisor	www.TripAdvisor.com – then search for Dijon or other town of interest. One of the best overall travel sights with details and reviews on most attractions, restaurants, and hotels.

Helpful Online Resources

1-Dijon and Burgundy Area Websites.

Website Name	Website Address and Description
US News	Travel.USNews.com – then search for Burgundy. Details on the weather and when to visit, area transportation, and hotels to consider.
You Tube	Several helpful videos available. One of the best is under the search term "Places to see in Dijon."
Visit French Wine	www.VisitFrenchWine.com – then go to the section on Bourgogne. Details on the area's wines, vineyards, area wine tours, and classes.
Wikipedia	En.Wikipedia.org – then search for Dijon. One of the best resources for the history of a town, its climate, and geography.
Wine Folly	www.WineFolly.com Guide to Burgundy wine, wineries, and tours.

2-Transportation Information and Tickets

Website Name	Website Address & Description
Burgundy Bike	www.BurgundyBike.com Bicycle rentals and tours for Dijon and the Burgundy region.
France Travel Planner	www.FranceTravelPlanner.com – then search for Dijon. Detailed information on most modes of transportation including area trains, trams, and the bus system.
French Train / SNCF	www.SNCF.com/en

2-Transportation Information and Tickets

Website Name	Website Address & Description
	Book rail tickets directly with French rail lines and find detailed information on time schedules and train availability.
Le Boat	www.LeBoat.com Canal boat rentals for the Burgundy region.
Train Ticket Resellers	Several services enable you to purchase train tickets online prior to your trip, including: - RailEurope.com - TrainLine.com - Eurorailways.com These sites are a good place to check schedules and train availability for all train companies servicing most areas in Europe.
Visio Train	www.VisioTrain.com Tour train for the town of Beaune.

3-Tour and Hotel Booking Sites

Company	Website address and description
Hotel Sites	Numerous online sites enable you to review and book hotels online. Most of these sites also resell tours. - Booking.com - Hotels.com - Expedia.com - Travelocity.com
Tour Resellers	Many companies, such as the ones listed here, provide a full variety of tours to Dijon

Helpful Online Resources

3-Tour and Hotel Booking Sites	
Company	Website address and description
	and Burgundy as well as day tours. The offerings are similar, but research is helpful as some firms offer unique services and tours. - GetYourGuide.com - ToursByLocals.com - Viator.com - WorldTravelGuide.net
Trip Advisor	www.TripAdvisor.com One of the most comprehensive sites on hotels and tours. Direct connection with Viator, a tour reseller.

Index

Apps to Download 6
Area Covered in the Guide 2
Attractions in Central Dijon ... 56
Autun, France Day Trip 109
Beaune Attractions 81
Beaune Cinema Mural 86
Beaune, France 79
Beaune, Lodging 87
Beaux Arts Museum 61
Besçancon Day Trip 110
Bicycle Rentals 48
Bicycle Tours 104
Boat Rentals 102
Botanical Gardens 76
Burgundy Life Museum 68
Burgundy Wine Route 97
Burgundy Wine Tours 99
Burgundy Wines 90
Chalon-sur-Saône 113
Cite de la Gastronomie 77
City Pass 39
Climate by Month 27
Darcy Park 69

Day Trips from Dijon 107
Dijon Cathedral 64
Dijon Owl 17
Divia Velodi Bicycles 48
Dole, France Day Trip 115
Dukes Palace 59
Events & Festivals 28
Fine Arts Museum 61
Gastronomy School 77
History of Dijon 15
Hospices de Beaune 82
Hotel Guide 31
Jardin Darcy 69
La Maison Maille 73
Le Boat.com 104
Les Halles Market 75
Liberation Square 58
Magnin Museum 66
Marina for Boat Rental 102
Mustard Boutiques 73
Mustard Shops 18
Natural History Museum 76
Notre-Dame Dijon 63
One Day Itinerary 3

Index

Owl's Trail 50
Place Darcy 71
Place de la Liberation 10, 58
Points of Interest List 56
Population Information 13
Produce Market 75
Rivers in Dijon 11
Rude Museum 67
Rue de la Liberte 73
Shopping Street 72
Sports Stadium 18
St. Benigne Cathedral 64

Tour Companies 43
Tour Phillipe 60
Tourist Office 4
Train Stations 20
Trams in Dijon 46
Unesco Sites 9
William Gate 71
Wine Capital of Burgundy 79
Wine Museum in Beaune 83
Wine Terminology 92
Wine Tours 99

Starting-Point Travel Guides

www.StartingPointGuides.com

This guidebook on Dijon is one of several current and planned *Starting-Point Guides*. Each book in the series is developed with the concept of using one enjoyable city as your basecamp and then exploring from there.

Current guidebooks are for:

Austria:
- Salzburg, and the Salzburg area.

France:
- Bordeaux, Plus the surrounding Gironde River region
- Dijon Plus the Burgundy Region
- Lille and the Nord-Pas-de-Calais Area.
- Lyon, Plus the Saône and Rhône Confluence Region
- Nantes and the western Loire Valley.
- Paris Day Trips by Train.
- Reims and Épernay the heart of the Champagne Region.
- Strasbourg, and the central Alsace region.
- Toulouse, and the Haute-Garonne area.

Germany:
- Cologne & Bonn
- Dresden and the Saxony State
- Stuttgart and the and the Baden-Württemberg area.

Spain:
- Camino Easy: A mature walker's guide to the popular Camino de Santiago trail.
- Toledo: The City of Three Cultures

Sweden:
- Gothenburg Plus the Västra Götaland region.

Switzerland:
- Basel & Bern, and nearby city and mountain adventures.
- Geneva, Including the Lake Geneva area.
- Lucerne, Including the Lake Lucerne area.
- Zurich – And the Lake Zurich area.

Fiction

Blue Water Bedlam

Murphy's Law has nothing on these guys!

Charlie just wanted to have some fun with his new boat and share that fun

Four retired guys set forth on a boating adventure north from the beautiful Puget Sound. Knowing nothing about what it takes to handle a yacht and the news of a recent murder on board doesn't stop them.

Camino Passages
Outdoor Adventure – Travel – Spain – Romance

The Camino de Santiago is an historical trail across northern Spain which provides hikers with an incredible variety of architectural, natural, and cultural delights. It also is, as Larry Adams learns, a wonderful social journey as well.

Setting out for Spain, Larry is only seeking a solo adventure and a much-needed change of pace. What Larry encounters during his walk are experiences and new relationships that could change his life forever.

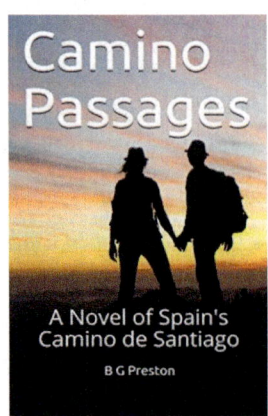

Obsidian Portal
A story of adventure and discovery. Four friends simply planned to kick back and relax, until half of a fish was found on the carpet.

Their simple discovery leads the group on an exciting quest. Have they uncovered a way to instantly transport people? They may have stumbled upon a whole new technology with astounding implications. Could it change the course of world economics and stir up a lot of trouble in the process?

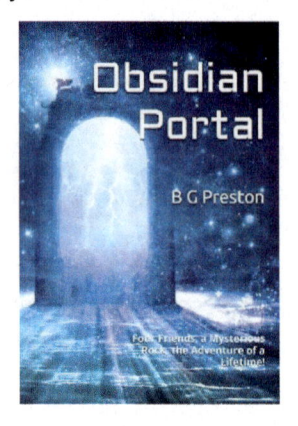

Books by B G Preston

Portal Lost

Adventure & survival in an untamed world.

A morning commute turns out to be far from normal when Amy Scott steps out from a portal to find herself in a strange world!

Portal Lost tells the exciting story of a band of hardy individuals who quickly change from living in a modern society to living in a rugged wilderness…or die trying.

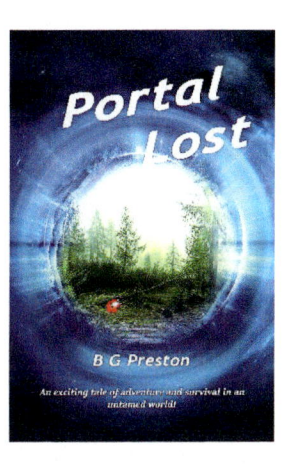

Updates on these and other titles may be found on the author's Facebook page at:

www.Facebook.com/BGPreston.author

Feel free to use this Facebook page to provide feedback and suggestions to the author or email to: cincy3@gmail.com

Printed in Great Britain
by Amazon